SHIPPING IN CHINA

Shipping in China

Edited by
TAE-WOO LEE
Korea Maritime University
MICHAEL ROE, RICHARD GRAY and MINGNAN SHEN
Institute of Marine Studies, University of Plymouth

Routledge
Taylor & Francis Group

LONDON AND NEW YORK

First published 2002 by Ashgate Publishing

2 Park Square, Milton Park, Abingdon, Oxon OX14 4RN
711 Third Avenue, New York, NY 10017, USA

Routledge is an imprint of the Taylor & Francis Group, an informa business

First issued in paperback 2016

British Library Cataloguing in Publication Data
Shipping in China. - (Plymouth studies in contemporary
   shipping and logistics)
   1. Shipping - China - History - 20th century
   I. Lee, Tae-Woo II. University of Plymouth. Institute of
   Marine Studies
   387 .5 ' 0951 ' 09045

Library of Congress Cataloging-in-Publication Data
Shipping in China / edited by Tae-Woo Lee ... [et al].
      p. cm. -- (Plymouth studies in contemporary shipping and logistics)
   Includes bibliographical references.
   ISBN 978-0-7546-1800-3
   1. Shipping in China. 2. Merchant marine--China. 3. Shipping--Government
policy--China. 4. Shipping--Government policy--Korea (South) 5.
Shipping--International cooperation. 6. Harbors--China. 7. Stevedores--China. I. Lee,
Tae-Woo. II. Series.

HE894 .S5 2002
387 .5'44'0951--dc21
                                                                2002074709
Transfered to Digital Printing in 2009

ISBN 978-0-7546-1800-3 (hbk)
ISBN 978-1-138-25822-8 (pbk)

Contents

Acknowledgments

Quite obviously, without the contributions of the authors this book would never have happened and so it is to them that many thanks must go. In addition there has been considerable support from my co-editors – Professor Tae-Woo Lee in Pusan, Dr Mingnan Shen in Dalian and Dr Richard Gray in Plymouth. Many thanks to them as well. Marie Bendell at the Institute of Marine Studies has provided her usual blend of encouragement and discipline which has been essential to the task in hand. In addition I am delighted to mention someone whom this last year has proved to be the closest of friends, a delightful personality and as open and warm as can be imagined – Lina Selkou – who has just spent an interesting year in Rotterdam and now has escaped back to Athens. She has provided more academic stimulus and social strength than I have ever met before and her sense of humour is both infectious and unrivalled. Wherever her next stopping point may be, I look forward to seeing her there one day.

And finally, as always, my family – Liz, Joe and Siân – deserve a special mention for their patience particularly with respect to the continued intrusion of football into their lives. Charlton Athletic, you all will be pleased to hear, remain successful, at least for the moment.

Michael Roe
Plymouth
September 2002

1 Introduction

Michael Roe
Institute of Marine Studies
University of Plymouth, United Kingdom

This book emerged from a long-standing close collaboration between the Institute of marine Studies, University of Plymouth in the United Kingdom and Korea Maritime University in Pusan, Korea which was first established in 1991 and since then has blossomed into a series of regular and frequent exchange visits of staff, joint research projects and collaborative publications. In addition to this, links between the two universities have led to a series of visits by Korean government officials from the Ministries of Transport and Maritime Affairs in Seoul along with an increasing number from allied institutions in China and in particular Dalian Maritime University.

This volume attempts to fill a yawning gap in the literature, which centres on the development of the maritime sector in China – a highly dynamic environment where the growth in the shipping and ports sectors has been nothing short of remarkable in the last 30 years. The papers presented here represent a cross-section of current views from experts in China, Hong Kong, Korea and Plymouth about the Chinese shipping industry and its links worldwide. Clearly the issues are too wide to be comprehensively discussed in one volume but it is hoped that within the text, there is sufficient discussion to give the reader a taste of the dynamism that characterises the market at the beginning of the new millennium.

The opening paper by Sun presents a discussion of the development of Chinese shipping policy and its wider impact and as such, provides a basis for many of the papers that follow. Work at Dalian University has been focussed on these issues for many years and this initial discussion provides a detailed and authoritative statement from an expert central to maritime policy-making in China.

This is followed by a more specific paper analysing the role of the sea-going labour market in China and its importance in the past with a closer look at its role as the industry develops. This is a particularly pertinent discussion given the problems that the developed countries are facing in terms of retaining and training sea-going labour and Sharma provides some detailed analysis of trends and policies that are likely to emerge in the coming years.

This is followed by the first of two papers by experts on the Chinese liner shipping industry – Shen and Lee – based in two different institutions and two different countries – Dalian and Pusan in China and Korea respectively. The first of their two papers focuses upon the development of COSCO (the Chinese state-owned liner shipping company) and how it has become a leading player in the container shipping market since the 1960s. Its role and importance are analysed and also its plans for the immediate future within the context of new policies emerging in general for the Chinese economy.

The paper by Song provides a detailed analysis of port competition between Hong Kong, where the author is based, and the area immediately adjacent in Southern China where some of the most dynamic developments in the region are taking place. Song provides a unique analysis of the relationships between these ports in the newly reunified China and also the potential for collaboration and co-operation between these ports in the coming years.

The significance of the trade in crude oil in China and Korea is analysed in the paper by Xinlian, Qingguang and Lee. The trading fleets are discussed and an attempt is made to go on and discuss the possibilities of co-operation between the two countries in this sector in both the trade and transportation area.

The second paper by Shen and Lee also looks at COSCO but now examines in some detail the effect of restructuring of the company during the period of economic reconstruction in China from the planned to the market economic system. Placing these developments in their economic context, Shen and Lee provide a unique commentary on the impacts of the macro changes in China at the company level from the perspective of experts from China itself and neighbouring Korea.

Meanwhile the paper by Roe examines the historical development of Polish-Chinese shipping relations from the early communist days of the 1950s through to the free market developments in both regions of the late 1990s and early 21st century. This trade was important as it represented the first international relationship between the new communist China and the outside world and is unique in that unlike all the other trades between East Europe and China, it is the only one to survive the traumas of the changes that have stemmed from the collapse of communism.

The paper by Chang is also an important contribution to research in that it analyses the close relationship that now exists between Chinese and Korean shipping interests and which is likely to develop further in the coming years. Despite a long history, this collaboration has only really taken off since 1979 and the opening of Chinese shipping interests to the outside world.

The final two papers consider two significant topics in the development of logistics and shipping in China in the coming years. Panayides takes a view from Hong Kong of the importance and growth of Foreign Direct Investment in the ocean shipping industry of China and its related sectors whilst Li Bao and Gray discuss the development of logistics in China with specific reference to the situation in Shanghai.

It is hoped that this text will provide stimulus to the shipping and logistics industry in China and its region and provide the basis for extended discussion amongst practitioners, policy-makers and academics of the issues which will undoubtedly develop over the coming years.

2 Chinese Shipping Policy and the Impact of its Development

Guangqi Sun and Shiping Zhang
Dalian Maritime University,
Dalian, People's Republic of China

Introduction

Since the foundation of the People's Republic of China, the Chinese policy related to contemporary shipping has been concerned with the international shipping community. Until now there has been no systematic report on this subject which is difficult to understand. The purpose of this paper is to fill this blank in policy research.

It is the case that Chinese shipping has an important position in the world in the 21st century. The reappearance of China's ocean fleet after the seven sailings to the West by Zheng He during the Ming Dynasty in the 15th century, has no doubt benefited from the encouragement and assistance of China's international shipping policy. It has also been a tortuous and frustratingly slow process and reflected the corresponding characteristics of both the era and the country.

In order to describe simply and conveniently Chinese shipping policy, it is convenient to divide it into two periods. The first is the period of China's planned economy (from October 1949 to 1978), whilst the second period is from the implementation of the open policy of China – that is the gradual change from the socialist market economy (from 1979 to now and which continues).

China's Shipping Policy for the Period of the Planned Economy (1949-1978)

In a similar fashion to the former USSR and other traditional socialist countries, China's shipping industry under the planned economy was essentially run and operated by the state in a collective manner. Since the government and enterprises were treated jointly as a combination of policy subject and object during this period, China's shipping policy mainly reflected protection and full support for ocean transport. In terms of specific development, it can also be divided into two parts: one was the initial development of the shipping industry through international co-operation and leasing foreign vessels; the other was the period of establishment of its own national ocean shipping fleet and the development of international shipping business.

The Background to Shipping Policy During this Period

Before the 1980s, the international shipping policy adopted by the Chinese government was on the basis of state-owned and collectively-owned shipping enterprises, working within a planned economy and centrally unified, administrative controlled model and policy system. The main reasons were as follows:

- At the beginning of the establishment of the new China, the western countries implemented a trade blockade and embargo policy. The new China had to operate its international shipping industry through the state to maintain the national economy and to promote reconstruction.
- At that time, China was influenced greatly by the former USSR, borrowing the highly centrally controlled, planning economic administrative model. Foreign trade cargoes were decided by intergovernmental department planning and control meetings. The state had the responsibility for international shipping including integration of government administration and enterprise management. The state bore both marine profits and losses.
- During the first 'Five-year Plan' between 1953 and 1957, China almost completed total socialist reform of privately owned industry and individual shipowners, establishing a state-owned, unitary public ownership and economic structure. The shipping industry, particularly the international shipping industry, was completely under the control of the state and shipping policies reflected the characteristics of a state-controlled and regulated, planned economy.

Measures to Initiate International Shipping Business

At the beginning of the 1950s, the newly established China had little opportunity to organise its own ocean fleet, since there were numerous other tasks to be undertaken. In order to recover the national economy as soon as possible, the Chinese government took the following measures to develop foreign trade transport, including the initiation of shipping business.

International co-operation in shipping Due to the trading block by the western powers, partners for the Chinese government in terms of trade co-operation could only be the socialist countries in the early 1950s, and the first was to take action was Poland where the state set-up a relatively strong link in shipping. On 15 June 1951, the governments of China and Poland set up the Chinese-Polish Joint Stock Shipping Co, in Tianjin (China) with a branch office in Gdynia (Poland) with the governments as the only shareholders following a proposal by Poland. The vessels flew the Polish flag. In July 1951, the Chinese government signed an agreement that Czechoslovakia was entrusted to operate two ocean-going vessels. The so-called entrustment of operation meant that Chinese vessels were fully operated by the Czechoslovakian authorities. China only provided a certain number of the seafarers. In terms of financial administration, Czechoslovakia settled accounts annually and took 3 per cent of the total revenue from service operation.

Leasing vessels In September 1950, the Chinese government established another international shipping company in Tianjin. The company was moved to Beijing in August 1952. The main task of the company was to develop foreign trade transport with vessels leased from overseas. In order to encourage enthusiasm from overseas and merchants to participate in foreign trade transport, the Ministry of Communications of the People's Republic of China took measures so that overseas Chinese individuals who had vessels, could act as private seagoing vessel agents. It stated that any property right designated to overseas Chinese or all the vessels of the Chinese merchants which flew foreign flags or held approval issued by the governmental overseas affairs commission, would enjoy preferential treatment.

Unification of operation and management of vessel agencies With the development of international co-operation in shipping and leasing foreign vessels, international merchant vessels calling at Chinese ports increased dramatically. In order to enhance their management, on 1 January 1953, the Shipping Management Bureau of the Ministry of Communications set up an ocean transport section – the China Foreign Ship Agent Company. All the vessels operated on international routes and those to and from Hong Kong, Macao and Taiwan, passing through Chinese waters and trading ports were served by this company in terms of immigration, customs declaration, visas, pilotage, anchoring, loading and discharging, passenger transportation services, insurance, survey, supply and rescue, maritime case handling and vessel chartering. The existing few foreign merchants and private agents ceased their business during the second half of 1955 and handed over their company activities to the state By 1960 the work was completed.

Setting up a tariff system The shipping recession in 1957 made the international freight costs of leasing vessels and the revenue from liner operations decrease sharply. At that time, the Chinese government launched a fierce war on tariffs with liner conferences in order to safeguard their interests. In coastal transport, the Chinese government declared on 12 February 1958:

- repeal of unfair tariffs that liner conferences had agreed for the transport of Chinese cargoes;
- implementation of the new tariff adopted by China.

In terms of ocean-going routes, the rates war lasted for a long time. Liner conferences were forced to reduce tariffs on the Far-East/European lines by about 30 per cent in 1959 until 1966, when the China Ocean Shipping Company adopted the 'China Ocean Shipping Tariff' and the disagreement ended. From then on China set up an independent ocean shipping tariff system.

The Policy Measures Adopted to Develop the Shipping Industry

At the end of the 1950s, the international situation improved day by day. With the cancellation of the international embargo policy upon China, the Chinese national economy developed rapidly and the international shipping policy of the Chinese government started to turn to one of establishing a national and domestic ocean shipping fleet to speed up the development of China's shipping industry.

Setting up state-owned ocean-going enterprises and an ocean shipping fleet
In 1958, the total marine transport volume of foreign trade had reached 11.58 million tons, some five times as high as it was in 1952. Only 20 per cent of the total volume of cargoes was shipped by the Chinese industry in accordance with foreign trade contracts, whilst some 60 per cent of this was transported by vessels hired from foreign countries. According to statistics for 1958 and 1959, annual leasing tonnage was over 1 million. This resulted in losing a large amount of foreign currency and also gave control to others both politically and economically. It was thus difficult to protect the national interest. At the same time, the Chinese shipbuilding industry developed gradually and cargo ships built by Chinese shipyards were ready to be introduced. Without a national ocean shipping fleet, the ships built could not sail in international waters, flying the Chinese national flag. Therefore, with the encouragement of the Ocean Transport Bureau of the Ministry of Communications, which was established in 1958, the Chinese government decided to accelerate the work of setting up its own shipping enterprises and ocean shipping fleet. On 27 April 1961, the China Ocean Shipping Company (COSCO), as well as COSCO Guangzhou Branch, was formally established. This opened a new chapter in the history of China's shipping industry.

Granting loans for purchasing vessels and establishing a state-operated shipping fleet The development of an established ocean fleet with leased vessels was relatively slow. Until 1962, transport capacity was only 140,000gt which represented only about 1 per cent of the total foreign trade volume. Therefore the transport of foreign trade was mainly undertaken by leased vessels at that time. Leasing foreign vessels took up a large amount of foreign currency. According to state statistics of the time, the costs of chartering vessels was as much as 383 million US$ from 1958 to 1962. This amount of money, at 1962 value, could purchase about 40 new vessels of 10,000gt or in total, more than 1 million gross tonnage. At that time, the international shipping market was in recession and the price of second-hand vessels was continuously decreasing. In the meantime, the surplus of international shipbuilding capacity was about 30-40 per cent and shipyards were providing advantageous loans to encourage orders: e.g. prepaid 10-30 per cent of the price of the vessel and the rest repaid within 7-10 years plus 5-6 per cent interest. The Chinese government judged the situation correctly and adopted the important, strategic decision of developing the shipping industry. In November 1963, the Chinese government decided to purchase second-hand vessels with the floating capital of the Bank of China, and developed an ocean shipping fleet. From then on, the development of China's ocean shipping fleet entered into a new period of development with loans to purchase vessels. Therefore, China's shipping industry grew rapidly. In 1975, the total tonnage of the ocean-going fleet was more than 5 million and in 1976 the total volume shipped by the Chinese fleet was about 70 per cent of the total foreign trade volume. This not only ended the pattern of relying on leasing foreign vessels for ocean transport but also laid a solid foundation for the open policy and reform period to promote China's shipping industry.

The Historical Functions of Shipping Policy During this Period

Generally speaking, Chinese international shipping policy before the period of reform and adoption of the open policy was in accordance with the national situation and conformed to economic developments, giving impetus to the growth and development of the Chinese international shipping industry. For example, during the 1950s, if China had not acted in a state capacity to begin co-operation in the leasing of vessels, it would not have realised the necessary progress in foreign trade transportation to meet the needs of the national economy. Another example is that at the end of the 1950s, with the continuous development of the national economy, the total amount of foreign trade transportation increased rapidly. If this transportation had relied mainly upon foreign vessels, it would have been obviously inappropriate. Therefore, taking advantage of the existence of a series of depressions in the shipping and shipbuilding markets, China purchased vessels with cheap loans and established an ocean-going fleet whilst adopting a series of preferential and supporting policies to promote its rapid growth. Precisely because of this, up to 1975, the total dead weight tonnage of the Chinese ocean-going fleet reached 5 million, undertaking 70 per cent of foreign trade cargoes, which basically ended the period of cargoes shipped dominantly by foreign vessels.

Since international shipping was operated entirely by the state, without doubt there was a shortage of economic pluralities and the planned economic pattern could not reflect the real market demand. Therefore, before the period of reform and open policy, the Chinese international shipping industry could only be operated as planned transport under national protection. The whole fleet was also made up of ageing vessels, of an unsuitable composition, outmoded technology, rigid management and lack of economic vigour and market competition.

China's Shipping Policy Since Reform and Opening to the Outside World (1978-present)

Since the implementation of reform and the open policy from 1978 and further development particularly in transition from a planned to a market economy, China has also reformed the state-owned shipping enterprises undertaking international marine transport. This reform can be divided into five steps: delegating power and making the enterprises more profitable (1978-1984), reforming the system from profit to taxation (1984-1986), changing the system of job responsibility through operation by contract (1987-1991), transforming the operational system (1991-1995) and experimenting in establishing a modern enterprise system (1995-2000 continuing). Reform of China's shipping policy therefore, formed a continuous system with historical origins in the planned economy but with obvious contemporary differences.

The Background to the Shipping Policy Adopted During the Transition Period to the Market Economy

Since the 1980s, Chinese international shipping policy has changed greatly. The basic reason for these important historical changes is that the whole country has concentrated upon economic construction and the entire national economic system has been changed from one of a planned economy to one of a market economy. The whole country under the national policy of reform and opening up has been gradually inter-mingled with the world economy and market. This has occurred particularly as follows:

- Separation of government and enterprise. International shipping enterprises have assumed sole responsibility for their profits and losses, become responsible for their independent development and established a modern enterprise system moving towards the development of a real independent market profile. Particularly at the end of the 1990s, the state decided that the enterprises under the Ministry of Communications and other institutions were to be separated from them. Thus the pace of Chinese international shipping enterprises moving towards legal responsibility, internationalisation and marketability was accelerated, resulting in international shipping policy derived for a planned economy to lose its main objectives. The whole policy system was moved towards further openness and freedom.

- Facing the new situation after joining the WTO. The new situation created by joining the WTO, which requires international shipping policy to be fully in tune with international shipping regulations and the practices of the WTO and GATS, has changed many things. China has participated in the GATS maritime negotiations since the beginning of the 1990s and kept to the required timetable for market access.

- The change of administration. The administration of the Chinese government of international shipping enterprises has changed from direct to indirect control and from one of administration to service. The functions of the government are mainly to adopt a macro-developmental strategy, to help in ensuring that real market information is available, to carry technology replacement forward, to strengthen training and to assess the qualifications of personnel involved in the industry. Although all these activities are macro-policy controls, it will also increase the competitive abilities of international shipping enterprises and help to ensure a better service geared towards the agents of economic re-construction and national modernisation.

The Adjustment and Development of Shipping Policy

Shipbuilding and Purchasing

Since 1978, and in particular since the transition of the national planned economic system towards the market economy, the national policy regarding state shipbuilding and purchasing vessels has made significant changes. In 1981, the Chinese government decided that any shipping enterprises which implemented an independent accounting unit and had the ability to repay the loan, including the basic investment of building and purchasing vessels, were allowed to move arrangements from those of the existing, planned financial allocation to one of enterprise loans. However, it was considered that commonly, shipping enterprises have marginal profits and it was often difficult to repay loans on time, so the government decided in 1984 that banks would provide low interest loans for building and purchasing vessels. In addition, they extended the time limit for repaying loans as well as reducing customs taxation.

Taxation Policy

During 1978 and 1979, the Ministry of Communications implemented the enterprise funding system for all state-owned shipping enterprises directly under the Ministry. That is, the enterprises could draw 5 per cent of total salaries as an enterprise fund if it fulfilled the overall designed production, quality profile and safety criteria designated by state.

From 1983 to 1985, the first step of a system of profit and taxation taking place at the same time was implemented. During the process of changing from profit to taxation, that is after an enterprise paid designated tax (normally 55 per cent), the profit after taxation could be allocated in three different forms – these were according to an increasing rate, a fixed proportion and adjusting tax rate – or the rest could all remain with the enterprise.

In 1986, the second step – taxes used as profit – was implemented, that is an enterprise could realise its profits and keep them with the enterprise after it had paid the state all necessary taxes. In 1994, the taxation system was reformed, the above-mentioned privileged policy was abolished and income tax was unified to 33 per cent. Unless there was a special exception, an enterprise could not enjoy income tax reduction privileges.

Cargo Reservation Policy

China is the largest developing country in the world and its cargo policy can be divided into two parts: cargo reservation and non-cargo reservation. Before the 1980s, China implemented a policy of national cargoes to be transported by national vessels. Generally speaking, Chinese foreign trade cargoes were allocated by the relevant departments and the individual shipping company just implemented the national plan for transport. At the same time, the Chinese government signed contracts on bilateral trade and transport with a number of relevant countries including clauses relating to cargoes reserved for Chinese ships. During this period, the shipping enterprises were also encouraged to acquire cargoes by themselves for their operation. However despite this policy of cargo direction by the state, the national foreign trade cargo share was still only 60 per cent.

From 1988, in order to comply with international practice, the Chinese government abolished the policy of national cargo transported by national ships. The government deregulated the shipping companies, both domestic and overseas operators, freeing up the carriage of Chinese import and export foreign trade cargoes. As a result, national shipping companies turned to acquiring cargoes through the free market. Meanwhile, cargo owners could also choose the carriers they wanted and at the same time tariff controls were also relaxed and were from then on decided by the market. At present, China only has reserved cargoes for trade with countries that previously signed maritime agreements.

Operational Subsidy Policy

The operational subsidy policy in China remains unclear and it is difficult (if not impossible) to find specific provisions or regulations. This is because during the period of the planned economy before 1980, the losses incurred by state-owned shipping enterprises were assumed by the state. Therefore the idea of a specific subsidy did not really exist. Since the policy of openness and reform has been adopted, Chinese state-owned shipping enterprises have been part of the process of the market economy and gradually have assumed sole responsibility for both profits and losses.

Market Access

Market access is a major component of the adjustment in China's international shipping policy. The Chinese government has continuously adopted and promulgated a series of new policies concerning market access according to the general trends within international shipping practice in order to accelerate the development pace of a modern international shipping industry within the country. The major components are as follows.

The policy relating to transport services In April 1985, the Chinese government adopted regulations that allowed foreign capital shipping enterprises to access the market of Chinese international transport in the form of a joint venture with approval of administrative measures for shipping companies engaged in international marine transport. In June

1990, the Ministry of Communications declared a set of regulations for international liner transport, and since 1st July 1990, foreign international shipping companies have been allowed to engage in the operation of international liner transport in Chinese ports. With respect to national treatment, there would be no discrimination between domestic or international companies. The Ministry of Communications further regulated in March 1992, under the principle of equality, that foreign shipping companies were to be allowed to establish sub-divisions through bilateral agreement for activities of shipping business. In July of the same year, foreign shipping companies were allowed to set up their own company or joint shipping enterprises. In terms of activities within China, they could engage in canvassing cargoes, issuing bills of lading, settling accounts and signing contracts related to shipping business for their own vessels. In November 1992, the Chinese government reaffirmed that foreign shipping companies were allowed to establish independent joint companies in China and could canvass cargoes, sign bills of lading, settle accounts and sign contracts for their own vessels. In September 1993, the Chinese government submitted revised quotations and a list of remitted most privileged treatment: with the aim of opening up China's shipping markets, the relevant foreign shipping companies could establish independent enterprises or sub-companies in China to engage in normal business activities.

Foreign shipping companies should have the following qualifications for establishing independent shipping companies in China: (1) more than 15 years experience in shipping and have a shipping office for more than 3 years in the city intended to set up a company; (2) the liner vessels should call at the port where the companies are intended to be set up every month; and (3) the registered capital of the foreign companies should be not less than 1 million US$. Operational scope: canvassing cargoes, signing bills of lading, settling tariffs, signing contracts for their companies and operated vessels.

Port service From 1st April 1992, the Chinese government unified port dues, loading and discharging fees, for both Chinese and foreign registered vessels occupied on international shipping to ensure that there was no discriminatory treatment. On 21st January 1994, the new Port Dues Regulation (Foreign Trade) was officially promulgated by the Ministry of Communications. All vessels, Chinese or foreign registered, were required to implement the new unified port dues and the foreign companies had to settle their accounts in foreign currency at the rate specified by the Bank of

China. Thus foreign vessels enjoyed national treatment for port services benefiting from harmonisation of port service provision in Chinese harbours.

In order to deepen and enlarge reform and accelerate the development of the transport industry, in July 1992, the Ministry of Communications promulgated a series of policies for market access, including encouraging the operation of public berths in port construction. This provided for the joint co-operation of Chinese and foreigners in loading and unloading at ports, cargo storage, packing and unpacking and relevant domestic road transport; allowed the Chinese and foreign companies jointly to lease terminals; allowed foreign merchants to invest and build special cargo terminals and specialised berths for cargo-owners; allowed foreign merchants to invest and operate land, and within the land area, allowed the construction and operation of specialised terminals.

Affiliated services to the shipping industry In December 1990, the Chinese government restated in 'The Chinese Container Administration of International Marine Transport' the process of approval of establishing international container transport enterprises, and also promulgated that with approval, foreign merchants were allowed to establish international container handling enterprises in Chinese ports in the form of co-operation; foreign merchants were also allowed to set up inland container freight terminals. In terms of domestic operators, there would be neither discrimination nor privileges. In July 1992, the Chinese government regulated that foreign merchants were allowed to operate loading and discharging logistics in the form of co-operation with state approval.

At this time, the Chinese government clearly declared that foreign enterprises were not allowed to operate shipping agent businesses independently but did allow foreign merchants to undertake freight forwarding. On 22nd February 1995, the Ministry of Foreign Economy and Trade promulgated in the document entitled 'Foreign Merchant Investment in International Freight Forwarding', the process of approving the details of foreign merchant investments in freight forwarding. The investors should be enterprises related to international freight forwarding and with a history of international freight forwarding for more than three years. They should have related managerial and specialised personnel, have steady cargo resources and possess a specific number of freight forwarding networks. The minimum registered capital was not less than 1 million US$. With approval, they could canvass, book, charter, operate international multimodal transport, logistics, container packing and unpacking, issue bills of lading, customs declaration, inspection, insurance, settle accounts for freight in trade and operate an international freighting forward agency for cargo imports and exports.

In addition to the above-mentioned marine transport services, China also implemented policies for coastal and inland water transport services similar to many countries in the world, including some elements of protectionism. The Chinese government also allowed foreign companies to develop water transport enterprises jointly with Chinese companies engaged in coastal and inland water transport.

The Historic Functions of International Shipping Policy During This Period

Increasing the competitive capabilities of Chinese international shipping enterprises within the international shipping market will enhance national shipping strengths. By the end of the 20th century, the total tonnage of the Chinese ocean-going fleet was 36 million dwt. ranking fifth in the world. The China Ocean-going Shipping Company (Group) (COSCO) is amongst the ten top liner operators in the world, whilst China Shipping Group is among the top 20.

The Chinese market is to be further opened and as a result, foreign shipping companies will come to China in increasing numbers. All shipping companies amongst the top 20 have established branches in China. Up to 2000, there were more than 50 foreign capital shipping companies, whilst joint shipping companies numbered more than 120, in addition to 360 foreign shipping offices. More than 30 shipping companies have opened container lines within Chinese ports.

The improvement and enhancement of the administration of the Chinese government transportation authority with particular regard to the shipping industry has also continued to take place. Since 1978, the modification of Chinese international shipping policies has changed the relationship between government and enterprises. The governmental administration has moved from one of enterprise management to that of industrial administration, from micro-management to macro-management, from direct management to indirect management. The administration of the government is now through rules, regulations and laws, making governmental authority more transparent and resulting in a significant increase in public confidence.

Conclusion

At present, Chinese international shipping policy continues to be modified and perfected, a series of International Shipping Regulations are still to be published and the Shipping Law continues to be drafted along with the Shipping Law and Seafarers Act. Hopefully together, these will move the Chinese international shipping industry towards a splendid new era.

References

Guangqi, S. (1998) *The International Shipping Policy*, Dalian Maritime University Press: Dalian.

The Ministry of Communications of the People's Republic of China (1999) *China Shipping Developments Report 1998*, Renmin Jiaotong Press, July.

The Ministry of Communications of the People's Republic of China (2000) *China Shipping Developments Report 1999*, Renmin Jiaotong Press, July.

The Ministry of Communications of the People's Republic of China (1985-1999) *The Collection of Transportation Regulations of the People's Republic of China*, Renmin Jiaotong Press.

3 The Sea-going Labour Market in the People's Republic of China and its Future[1]

Krishan Kumar Sharma
Eurasia Group of Companies, Hong Kong

Introduction

The turn of the century has brought new opportunities and challenges for the shipping industry. One of the toughest challenges concerns the supply of good quality seafarers and in many ways it is at its lowest point presently. Having exhausted traditional supply sources, ship-operators are looking at alternative manning sources. The People's Republic of China (PRC) in this regard, has attracted the highest attention from the major industry players. In this paper, after describing the basic nature of seafaring, the trends in the Sea-going Labour Market (SGLM) worldwide are examined and the factors that make successful seafarers. In this context, developments in the PRC's SGLM and the role of the various actors concerned with the SGLM in the PRC are also described. In conclusion, some of the required initiatives from the main players in PRC's SGLM are specified.

The Nature of Seafaring

Seafaring is, in its most part, not possible to compare with shore based occupations. Seafaring generally means sailing on ships in excess of six months in complete isolation from society. In its most general context, a ships' complement can be viewed as officers and ratings often collectively called crew. Looking at this in more detail, the ships' complement can be

---

[1] Views expressed in this article are the author's and do not reflect the views of organisations with which he has been associated in the past or present in any way.

viewed as five clear segments – Deck Officers, Engine Officers, Deck Crew, Engine Crew and Galley Crew. Consider a ship with a complement of 20, none of the groups have more than five persons each. This exemplifies the social isolation with which a seafarer is faced when he steps on the gangway to sign the article of agreement.

On ships, the work group and social group are not an outcome of composition selected from an individual choice but stem from the time of day, the ships' operational requirement and the manner in which the supply chain in the SGLM works. For example a third engineer works under direct orders of the second engineer in the work setting of the engine room, but may have a joking relationship in the smoke room. A second engineer may be highly demanding in the engine room with his subordinates, but he may be very friendly in city visits while the ship is in a port. A chief engineer may be best friends with the master but rarely will ever get to sail with him again. On the other hand a third engineer may work very closely with an oiler due to the interdependent nature of the work in the engine room but may not have any opportunity to interact with the same person beyond the work setting. He is forced to either interact with the second officer as they share the same watch or remain alone and aloof.

Work complexity on ships is unmatched. Present day technological advances have fuelled this. Besides the fundamental characteristics of seafaring with the historical legacy of adventure associated with it, the general reduction in crew complements is the major cause of increased work complexity. Consider a master's position on the ship; whilst discharging his legal responsibilities, he also has to protect crew, owner, reputation and the public at large. Often these demands can be conflicting where a lot of managerial and diplomatic skills are required whilst retaining the highest levels of integrity. On the ship itself, a master who has risen through the navigational cadre has to immediately shun that affiliation as he moves from chief officer's role to that of master, a difficult task indeed, which many would find a problem to achieve in practice. Present day masters command ships more or less as complex as present day oil refineries or factories with 20 crew on board. Similarly his counterpart chief engineer has to work in excess of 20 complex and integrated systems and thousands of pieces of live equipment at any one time. If he does not have spares, he has to fabricate them in many cases or manage without them. The nature of complex work is not only restricted to the highest levels alone within the shipboard hierarchy; when an Able Bodied Seamen decides where to stand when a ship is being pulled by a shore line, he is making as big a decision as saving his life.

Complexity in the seafaring profession is not restricted to work alone. It permeates to the level of human interactions. Apart from the divided occupational specialisations that exist in seafaring, it is a common scenario to have a multi-national crew on board with diverse work values, culture, training and orientation. For example, this might include a Filipino Oiler reporting to a Pakistani Bosun, who is under the charge of an Ukrainian Second Engineer reporting to a British Chief Engineer, themselves under the command of a tired Indian Master faced with frequent calls and numerous emails from the ship's manager, charterer and owner in the absence of an erstwhile Purser or Radio Officer. Strong departmental affiliations across deck and engine departments add further to this complexity in the organisational structure on board. On the other hand there are numerous suppliers to the ship and the ship has to interact with several authorities and organisations many of them statutory or having substantial powers in relation to ships' operations. Generally the only means for an individual seafarer to draw emotional support is through the telephone line by occasional calls to home through the ship's satellite telephone. As a result, each individual on the ship is faced with demanding and complex human interactions that are unmatched in any shore based occupations.

The Sea-going Labour Market

Indeed seafaring is unique and that is one of the reasons seafarers command a special status ashore. However, it is not only seafaring that commands a special status ashore but also the nations themselves with significant numbers within the SGLM.

Historically, the manning of ships has moved from traditional supply sources typically from the western world to non-traditional countries like India, Philippines, Indonesia, etc. Whereas in the 1960s and 1970s it was USA and UK that ruled the SGLM, along with Norway, Germany and other European countries, in the 1980s and 1990s countries such as India and the Philippines have become the undisputed leaders of the SGLM. The manning of ships has strong 'footprints', and has moved from one country to another after exhausting the seafaring resources. Simultaneously many other things have changed. The technology of ships has become much more complex, the ship's complement smaller, voyages shorter due to increased speed and port stays have become negligible as a result of faster turnaround. Many of these changes have had a fundamental impact on the work of seafarers, the nature of seafaring and the overall attractiveness of the occupation to an individual. Moreover, as a result of economic development and higher levels of commerce in home countries, a potential entrant to the seafaring occupation has more occupational choices than ever before.

Against this backdrop, the beginning of the 21st century is in many ways a turning point in the composition of the SGLM. The elusive question in the year 2001 is which of the traditional supply sources are going to remain viable and which are going to emerge as the new leaders? Academicians and practitioners have been debating this issue for a number of decades now. Increasing attention has been placed in the last decade upon the first serious attempt to understand the demographics of the SGLM initiated by ISF in 1990. Two more attempts down the line, the questions still looms large – who will man the world fleet? While, many alternative hypotheses have been proposed such as India, the Philippines or Eastern European countries, any of which could be leaders in one or more of SGLM segments, logically it cannot be denied that PRC is definitely in every list. This is because there are certain broader but fundamental reasons that ensure adequate supply to a typical labour market like the SGLM. Three major reasons are the population of the country, the training infrastructure and the availability of alternative occupational opportunities. PRC naturally holds the lead in all of them to ensure that adequate supply is maintained to the SGLM.

The only doubts that have been cast on its non-sustainable supply to the SGLM are the weak communication skills of the PRC seafarers in English and to a lesser extent lower occupational tenure of the PRC seafarers. History has shown that it does not take long to pick up a language. All that is required is the right environment and conscious efforts. On the other hand efforts from all concerned in shipping in PRC have placed adequate stress in building communication skills in English. In terms of occupational tenure, historically India has had the lowest occupational tenure especially of engineer officers, but it is its engineers who still hold the key positions in shipowning and ship-management companies all over the world. It is indisputable that Indian seafarers command a premium in the SGLM until now and as long as there is adequate supply of similar seafarers from India, they will continue to do so. Therefore, whether it is right or wrong, lower occupational tenure does not preclude any nation from leading the SGLM.

The arguments against any nation leading the SGLM will continue even if a country clearly leads in numbers such as the Philippines. It is probable that there will never be a clear winner on all the human resource dimensions of the SGLM. Notwithstanding this, it is expected that seafarers from countries like the Philippines, India and PRC would be at the forefront of the SGLM at least for a few more decades.

Assuming that PRC is going to be one of the leaders in its supply to the SGLM, the next question that comes to mind is what is the role of PRC seafarers in the SGLM? It is important to note that this question is equally valid for any other nation that wants to lead the SGLM. This is so because the nature of seafaring is a given thing and is independent of any national characteristic. It is the seafarers that adapt to the sea and not the other way round.

Characteristics of an Ideal and Typical Seafarer

Characteristics of an ideal and typical seafarer are independent of their nationality. Therefore, the following description is equally applicable to PRC, Indian, Filipino or any other national in a seafaring occupation.

The requirements of multifunctional knowledge are typical of the seafaring specialisation – engineering or navigation – unlike its many counterparts ashore that require narrow specialisation. For example, a marine engineer has to acquire knowledge of engineering disciplines such as mechanical, electrical, naval architecture, electronics and instrumentation, beyond the applied core of marine engineering. Apart from this he has to learn core concepts of shipbuilding, commercial operations of ships, basics of navigation and seamanship and fundamentals of international trade and economics. To apply what one learns in the core components of mechanical engineering courses, there is a very big engine and a number of boilers on the ship. Even a simple turbocharger is a gas turbine. There is a complete power management system that operates at least two to three electrical generators. To put it simply, it is one of the rare professions where one can get an opportunity to apply all of what the student has learnt in his college. And one has to learn a lot at college and constantly update this knowledge at sea. This occupation requires from its practitioners to either learn or stagnate. Occupational licensing enforces this regime, such that you cannot become a second engineer unless you clear exams for that rank, you cannot become a chief engineer unless you clear exams for that. And you cannot be considered for occupational licensing unless you gain a minimum experience in running a ship.

While marine engineering requires a lot of theoretical inputs and skill acquisition, navigation is more a skill-based occupation. As such in any seafaring occupational specialisation, knowledge in itself is not sufficient; one has to have skills to apply that knowledge. For example, the theory of navigation is not going to help when one has to navigate the ship out at sea. Knowing how an engine operates does not overhaul the engine. So a seafarer is required to refine their skills and constantly acquire new ones to move on and upwards in the occupation.

The high level of requirements of knowledge and skills in seafaring occupations has several implications for seafarers and the nation that aims to provide seafarers to the SGLM. At an individual level, seafarers have to learn a lot before occupational entry and then constantly upgrade. They cannot afford to relax on ship, as they have to learn and apply this new knowledge besides performing routine jobs on ship. They have to teach their juniors. They have to mentor them. With limited numbers in the ships crew complement, sub-optimal performance by even one seafarer in the team puts tremendous burden on every one else. Clearly it is a profession for hands-on persons who thrive in a learning and applying environment.

A ship itself is worth several million dollars. Adding the value of cargo that it carries, its total worth is in hundreds of millions of dollars. On the other hand there could be several nationalities making up the crew composition, the ship may visit several countries in a month, may ride several rough seas and can journey for months not seeing land. Naturally it requires an attitude that helps one to face the toughest of challenges, complex work situations, cultural adjustments, hierarchical relationships, strict discipline and so on. Fundamentally, a seafaring occupation demands three things from its practitioners – safety of life on board, safe carriage of cargo and preservation of the ship and environment. Only the right attitude and habits can ensure this is achieved. A seafarer has to internalise the attitude and habits that help them discharge their duties professionally.

If a shipowner or a ship-manager were asked what kind of seafarer they would like to have on their ships, the characteristics noted above would describe their requirement in general terms. However, a seafarer also has certain typical aspirations from the seafaring occupation as well, which the shipowner or the ship-manager has to meet. A seafarer's typical aspirations in the short term, i.e. when signing on articles, is to do the job for the required time and get back to near and dear ones, safely, with contracted wages in their pocket or bank account. In the longer term there is a need to grow professionally and at a future date settle in a shore-based job. As long as they are seafaring, they are in the spot market that is characteristic of the SGLM. Their skills are valued equally by the shipowner or ship manager and performance is easily monitored on the ship. Wages are competitive and not very different from one employer to another, in general. Then what determines relations with the employer are typical short and long-term aspirations. In general, with 3-5 changes of employer in a career (generally spanning 12-15 years), there is achieved over time a match between their own and the employer's aspirations. Indeed high turnover is a characteristic of the SGLM, but then a seafarer is not in the firm's internal labour market, he is in the occupational internal labour market as long as they are seafaring.

Developments in PRC's SGLM

With a population of over 1.2 billion and with the SGLM size in excess of 350,000, PRC is one of the natural choices of ship-manning in the future. This is more so due to a clear public policy mandate to the export of labour to the SGLM, excellent maritime training infrastructure and strong entrepreneurial initiatives.

The PRC's Ministry of Communication is charged with managing the maritime sector. Supported by other provincial governments and their maritime organisations, the public policy mandate to ship manning enterprises is clear. This is made a clearer mandate due to the sub-conscious realisation that PRC missed the boat in the increasing numbers involved in the SGLM in the 1980s. Other obvious reasons are the need to create well paid jobs, economic conditions and household income and general support by the PRC as it becomes integrated into the world economy.

The maritime training infrastructure in the PRC is of the highest quality. The number of first rate maritime training institutions in China goes into double digits. Many of them are part of the university system of fully-fledged universities. Having visited some of them the general impression one gets is that they are excellent training grounds for future seafarers. A look at the industry trend shows that many other important maritime organisations concur with this view and have established collaborative arrangements with these institutions. For example, recently the Norwegian Shipowners Association set up a joint training facility with Shanghai Maritime Academy. Many manning companies in the PRC already have long-lasting partnerships with some of the leading maritime training institutes in the PRC. Some of the foreign shipowners have also invested in the training infrastructure of these institutes.

The entrepreneurial initiative to export to the SGLM, to say the least, is impressive. There are 39 manning organisations. Many of the big manning companies supply full complement in excess of 20 ships to at least one single owner and at any one point of time many of them have foreign clients in two digits. Even at provincial level there are excellent manning agencies that rival (and even have a bigger clientele of foreign shipowners and ship managers) the big manning companies. Although it is difficult to gauge the total number of potential maritime officer level graduates, some estimates by PRC manning experts suggest a number in the region of 6,000 per year. In any case, the number of quality maritime graduates is above 3,000 per year – at least 2,000 to man the more than 1,000 strong foreign-going vessel fleet and another 1,000 to supply foreign owners and coastal vessels. Many shipping companies have established relationships with manning agents and training institutions especially to recruit cadets. This is a robust testimony to the potent entrepreneurial drive of PRC's manning organisations.

Besides seizing an opportunity, one of the hallmarks of good entrepreneurial drive is realisation of limitations. Interestingly many of the manning agents one gets to meet, score high on that account. However, the biggest limitation of PRC manning is poor communication ability in English. To rectify this problem, a number of sophisticated language laboratories in most training centres have been set up and their is regular training prior to each new engagement of the crew as a part of manning infrastructure and refresher courses given to seafarers during their leave.

Manning constitutes around 45-50 per cent of total ship operating costs and as a result, the largest potential for cost-saving can come from this major cost centre. Whilst many nations are gradually pricing themselves out of the SGLM, the economic conditions as well as business itself in the PRC is not faced with similar pressures. The economic scenario in the interior of the PRC is even more conducive to attract quality seafaring trainees to the industry. Industry experts vouch that it is easy to get PRC seafarers at HK CBA, while for many countries one has to offer a premium above HK CBA. Overall many industry experts also feel that public policies in any other country are not as supportive to the seafaring occupation as they are in the PRC.

The Role of Actors Concerned with PRC Seafarers

There are three main actors concerned with PRC seafarers – government, PRC manning agents and training establishments, and foreign shipowners/managers.

The government on its part, is highly proactive in its support to the PRC's SGLM. The number of first rate training institutes for seafarers and investment in training is unmatched elsewhere. The government facilitates industry investment in the training infrastructure. Document requirement such as passport, visa and seafarers' discharge certificates are facilitated. Travel in and out of the PRC is relatively easy. Marketing of PRC seafarers is facilitated through seminars, conferences, regulation and support to manning agents. Overall, there is a positive public policy framework to support the PRC's SGLM in offering its services to foreign ships. Of course there are a few issues related to industrial relations that need to be resolved. It is expected that in years to come, things will be far better.

Manning agents all over the world are respected for their customer orientation and friendly approach. PRC manning agents are no exception to this. The difference between them and manning agents elsewhere is twofold. First the seafarers they place on ships outside PRC need to have good communication skills, which at present is the weakest link, thereby reducing marketability. Second, in general they are not part of any foreign ship-management or ship-owning firms, which means that first they have to adapt to the new ways of doing business and second they have no captive business to look for. So more than any other category of manning agents they have to put in extra effort. Indeed experience shows that they realise these limitations and are willing to walk the extra mile. Success of PRC supply to the global SGLM will largely depend how hard they work on known limitations in offering good quality seafarers to the outside world. Trends in their efforts in training their own seafarers suggest that they will certainly do the extra needed. In this regard, partnering of well-known maritime training institutions in PRC with manning agents is going to play a catalytic role. The realities of business life and the professional requirements of multi-national shipping companies are, to a certain extent, different from the national fleet that the PRC seafarers, manning agents, and training institutions are used to. For example, the difference in the numbers of crew complement on a foreign ship itself makes a substantial difference to the work-load, operational requirements and service level expected out of the seafarers. A multinational crew, apart from the demanding communication skills required, carries the additional burden of making cultural adjustments, reporting relationships and catering habits to name but a few. With changes in the manning scenario, it will be the first and prime responsibility of the training institutions to select the right candidates in the beginning and then train them in such a way that they are well adapted to the realities of international shipping right from the start. This is required irrespective of whether PRC seafarers work for domestic or international shipping companies in the future. With well-trained maritime graduates, manning agents will take on the next vital role in making it a success.

Many shipowners and ship-managers have put additional efforts in to recruit and train PRC seafarers. Looking at the history of manning, in the past both shipowners and ship-managers have put similar efforts in the case of other nations, so the PRC is no exception. But this time there is a difference. Over the years, trends show that the tonnage under ship-management has increased. The economics of ship operations definitely makes it easier for a shipowner to be more patient in their recruitment and training which to that extent is not possible with ship-manager's working on thin profit margins and severe competition for tonnage in its fleet. Hence they may not be as supportive. However, the balancing lever this time is the conditions of tight supply situations in the SGLM, where the shipowner and manager is faced with restricted choices never faced in the past to such an extent. It is expected that all actors concerned with PRC manning have to pitch in to make it a success, through patience, training, and collaborative efforts.

Opportunities Ahead for PRC Seafarers

Whilst various actors concerned with seafaring will do their bit in making PRC manning a success, it is the seafarers themselves who will have to walk the longest stretch in ensuring that it is indeed a success. First and foremost, communication skills are acquired skills and no amount of training can ensure that one can communicate well. As English is becoming a norm in international shipping it is the responsibility of the PRC seafarers themselves that they acquire this skill as quickly as they can during their fundamental training for the occupation. There are a variety of ways to do this, such as courses in English, extracurricular activities and exposure to the language. Since most of the maritime training establishments in the PRC are part of institutions of higher learning, opportunities to ensure that such an environment is created are plenty. But efforts finally have to come from the trainees themselves. For those PRC seafarers who sail the high seas, the right environment is already there to hone their communication skills. All they have to do is to utilise these opportunities whilst sailing with an international crew complement.

As seafaring is becoming more and more complex in its requirements, it is necessary that apart from having refined skills, new entrants as well as existing PRC seafarers have to have sound theoretical knowledge and constantly build upon it. The best way of building on existing knowledge is onboard training by seniors. A mentor's role in practice-based occupations such as seafaring is high and hence the role of seniors on-board becomes paramount. To make PRC manning a success, those PRC seafarers who are already working on foreign or domestic ships must take the initiative in training junior seafarers. This is equally applicable to non-PRC seafarers. The success of Indian manning apart from the good occupational entry training and a robust training and examination system, is largely based upon the responsibility taken up by senior seafarers. As in any mentor's case, they must ensure shipboard learning through appropriate actions and a hands-on approach to teaching, understanding the junior's needs and supporting them through easy and difficult shipboard tasks. Mentoring at its best means achieving the right blend of reward and reprimand, a reflection of a thorough professional and gentleman's approach and encouraging positive feedback. At the same time junior seafarers must take the initiative in learning and building a professional and knowledge-based practice within their occupation by learning from senior seafarers.

The tendency of short occupational tenure in seafaring has been a constant problem. It is feared that the PRC is not going to be an exception to that trend. As in every other occupation, seafaring has its own pleasures and pain. However, if viewed objectively, in comparison to much shore-based employment, seafaring is as good as many other occupations. Apart from the hardship of sailing away from home, it is one of those occupations that can provide opportunities for high levels of job satisfaction. The fragmented design of this occupation, the imbalances in the work-load and limited opportunities for progression in the occupation are definitely certain inherent flaws. But these are not new things in seafaring and have existed from the days of sailing ships. However, gradually things are changing for the better. For example, with the implementation of STCW 95, there are a variety of new opportunities that are likely to emerge such as alternative certification. The future role of PRC seafarers, or for that matter any seafarer, lies in seizing such opportunities as and when they arise. The role of public policy and the training institution will rest in fully exploring such opportunities and capitalising upon them as and when it is possible. In fact, out of all the nations supplying the global SGLM, the PRC is probably the one with the most robust training infrastructure – based upon the number of universities catering for the maritime sector – that can implement alternative certification, if it becomes a reality.

Seafaring often has been referred to as a 'calling'. Shore-based job opportunities do have an impact upon how many and the calibre of entrants that are attracted to seafaring. For example, if comparable jobs were available ashore, less and less people would want to go to sea. However at the same time, not all want to become doctors, lawyers or IT programmers. Any nation with a large population should be in a position to attract sufficient numbers to sea. The role of existing seafarers then becomes one of giving an objective assessment about the occupation to anyone interested. Whilst highlighting the bad points, it is also equally important to speak about the good points so that potential entrants can make an objective assessment about career choices. The role of public policy and training institutions is also important in establishing an objective and unbiased job preview of seafaring to new entrants. It is this joint effort that will first ensure that the right persons are attracted to the occupation and second, help in increasing the occupational tenure of those who eventually join the profession. The PRC, like India, has a significant advantage in its large population, which ensures that there would be no dearth of people who would like to join seafaring and make a long-term career out of it. On the other hand, the wrong selection and an improper job preview in the pre-training stage is a certain way to ensure high turnover (withdrawal) from the seafaring occupation.

Whilst seafaring is about sailing on the high seas, opportunities do not stop there for the best. After spending a reasonable period on-board ship, acquiring necessary knowledge and confidence, there are opportunities for such seafarers as and when they want to leave. Seafaring in itself is a large foreign exchange earner for any economy but there is an equally vibrant economy outside seafaring that is largely dependent upon ex-seafarers. The world of ship-management, shipowning, and other allied businesses are dependent upon those seafarers who make a mark as excellent seafarers. However, such opportunities are only open to the best and brightest, since supply far exceeds demand for such professionals. The role of a seafarer then becomes ensuring that he excels in seafaring so that he is able to make the switch when he wants. The role of public policy then is in ensuring that such seafarers are there, otherwise a complete segment of business cannot prosper within its portfolio of professions.

Conclusions

Manning for the world fleet of merchant vessels is standing at a crossroads. It is not certain which nation is going to take a lead in its supply to the SGLM. Given these uncertainties, there is high likelihood that the PRC will take a lead in manning the world fleet owing to public policy support, high entrepreneurial initiative and its good training infrastructure. The main reasons that bring uncertainty about PRC taking a lead are the low communication skills in English of PRC seafarers and their lower tenure in the occupation. Naturally, to make PRC manning a success it is important to consider that any amount of entrepreneurial initiative or government support cannot turn an under-qualified seafarer into an excellent seafarer. It necessarily involves clear vision and strategy and a willingness to commit resources and effort that has to come from within PRC resources. On the other hand it is also about time that all actors in the PRC concerned with its SGLM, consciously thought about what kind of culture they would like to build for the seafaring occupation because in the absence of joint and focused efforts, the culture that is likely to emerge is going to be one of accident and not design. Such a culture is not going to give PRC's SGLM the necessary edge, which it is close to achieving. It is in everyone's interest that PRC manning is successful as there are only a few countries in the world that have potential to man much of the world fleet. As economic conditions continue to improve further and further in these countries, the list of such countries continues to shrink.

Acknowledgments

I am thankful to the editors of this book for inviting me to write on this timely topic, to Amitabh Kumar Sharma for his valuable suggestions on the earlier drafts of this paper and to the Eurasia Group of Companies – my present employers – that provided me with an opportunity to work on PRC SGLM for an extended period of time. I have had the opportunity to meet several manning companies, and to visit maritime training centres and universities in the PRC in the past few years for which I am also grateful. My own understanding of SGLM is also a result of exceptional opportunities presented at the Indian Institute of Management, Ahmedabad as a Doctoral Scholar in Management, and earlier at the Directorate of Marine Engineering and Training, Calcutta and Bombay (now Marine Engineering Research Institute) as a Marine Engineering Cadet. My seafaring stint with ESSAR, GESCO and Denholm gave me a first hand perspective about seafaring. My thanks go to these institutions and organisations.

References

Asian Institute of Transport Development (1993) *Indian Shipping Industry: Critical Issues in Global Context*, New Delhi: AITD.

BIMCO/ISF (1995) *World-wide Demand For and Supply of Seafarers*, Warwick: The University of Warwick, Institute for Employment Research.

BIMCO/ISF (2000) *World-wide Demand For and Supply of Seafarers*, Warwick: The University of Warwick, Institute for Employment Research.

Dictionary of Occupational Titles (1991) (4th ed.) (Vols. 1-2). Washington, DC: US Government Printing Office.

Haralambides, H.E. (1991) An Econometric Analysis of Sea-going Labour, *The Logistics and Transportation Review*, 27(1), 15-31.

Helmick, J.S. and Glaskowasky, N.A. Jr. (1994) Regulatory Constraints on Innovative Manning Practices in US Flag Merchant Fleet, *The Logistics and Transportation Review*, 30(3), 284-301.

Hill, J.M.M. (1972) *The Seafaring Career*, London: Centre for Applied Social Research, Tavistock Institute of Human Relations.

Holland, J.L. (1976) Vocational Preferences, in Marvin D. Dunnette (ed.), *Handbook of Industrial and Organisational Psychology*, 521-545, Chicago: Rand McNally College Publishing Company.

IAMR (1973) *A study of Manpower Requirement for the Merchant Navy 1974-79*, IAMR Report No.4/1973, New Delhi: Institute of Applied Manpower Research.

International Maritime Organisation (1995) *STCW Conventions: Resolutions of 1995 Conference*, London: IMO.

ISF (1990) *ISF guide to International Maritime Labour Supply*, London: Lloyd's of London Press.

Price, J.L. (1977) *The Study of Turnover*, Iowa: The Iowa State University Press.

Roggema, J. and Smith, M.H. (1983) Organisational Change in Shipping Industry: Issues in the Transformation of Basic Assumptions, *Human Relations*, 36(8), 365-390.

Sharma, K.K. (1998) *Occupational Withdrawal: a Study of Indian MNOs in the International Shipping Industry,* unpublished doctoral dissertation, Indian Institute of Management, Ahmedabad.

Shimberg, B., Esser, B.F. and Kruger, D.H. (1973) *Occupational Licensing: Practices and Policies,* Washington, D C: Public Affairs Press.

Walton, Richard E. (1987) *Innovating to Compete: Lessons for Diffusing and Managing Change in the Work Place,* San Francisco: Jossey-Bass Publishers.

Williamson, O.E. (1981) The Economics of Organisations: the Transaction Cost Approach, *American Journal of Sociology,* 87(3), 548-577.

4 COSCO Development Strategy

Mingnan Shen
Shipping Management College
Dalian Maritime University
Dalian, People's Republic of China
Tae-Woo Lee
Division of Maritime Transportation Science
Korea Maritime University
Pusan, Korea

Introduction

Since its establishment in 1961, COSCO has developed to be one of the top ten shipping conglomerates in the world with its container fleet having grown to be number seven in terms of slot deployed. The purpose of this study is to examine COSCO's development strategy in the period of Chinese economic reform and analyse its effects on COSCO's development.

Before 1978, the development pattern and growth performance of a state-owned enterprise (SOE) in China largely depended on the central government's arrangement, which was strongly influenced by its politically driven strategy. In the shipping industry, the SOEs were simply subsidiaries of the Ministry of Communication (MOC) and many important decisions, particularly concerning the expansion of the fleet, were made directly by government departments. All profits earned by the enterprises were handed over to government, while all losses were underwritten by it (Wan, 1988a). The result of this was to make the main task of a shipping company to fulfil the state's plan. For instance, the objective of China Ocean Shipping (Group) Company (COSCO) was to serve China by carrying cargo thus earning foreign currency.

The open-door policy adopted by the Chinese government has made a great contribution to Chinese international trade over the past two decades. Due to the expansion of foreign trade, international transportation has become particularly important. According to statistical reports from the MOC, on average over 75 per cent of foreign trade is carried by sea annually. However, despite this significant growth in foreign trade, the shipping market has become highly competitive due to the emergence of numerous domestic and foreign ocean carriers. Faced with this increasingly competitive global market, COSCO has had to find ways to be more competitive. Since separating from the MOC in 1984, it has maintained the restructuring of its organisation and strategy and added as objectives the making of the best possible return on equity, maintaining the strongest possible cash flow, paying the company's taxes, being good and socially responsible corporate citizens and respecting the environment. In COSCO's 2001 working conference, a clear idea of its development strategy was given as strengthening shipping business, developing logistics and to access capital markets.

Today COSCO has emerged as a complete commercial entity based on Chinese Corporate Law and running independently in the market. It owns and operates one of the largest fleets in the world with about 500 ships comprising most types and of over 20 million dwt, trading to practically everywhere. The objective of this study is to examine COSCO's development strategy in the period of Chinese economic reform and analyse its effects on COSCO's development. Data was collected by literature survey and interviews with managers of COSCO and MOC.

Implementing Economic Contract Responsibility System (ECRS)

Reform of Chinese SOE has been a gradual and incremental process focused mainly on a progressive increase in managerial autonomy. Between 1984 and 1985 the enterprise income tax on state-owned enterprises was introduced and tax payments replaced profit remittances as the main source of fiscal revenue from enterprises. In turn the enterprises were allowed to retain most of their after-tax profits and their depreciation funds.

In 1986, after its successful experiments in the Chinese agriculture sector, ECRS (which permits enterprises' obligations to the government to be determined on the basis of contracts defining their output and profit remittances) was introduced to medium-sized and large SOEs on a nationwide basis.

In 1992, according to the Enterprise Law of 1988 and its implementing regulations, the Chinese government no longer interfered with the operations of enterprises and they were endowed with a set of 14 rights over their operations. However, they were expected to be accountable for their performance; inefficient and loss-making enterprises were to be restructured or closed down in accordance with the Bankruptcy Law of 1986 (Wan, 1988b). Since then ECRS has become an integral part of the enterprise to increase incentives for co-operation but with penalties for non-co-operation.

ECRS on Board

COSCO started its experiment with ECRS (taking it 'on board') since it was introduced to reform the Chinese agriculture sector in 1979 as an attempt to improve the economic efficiency of those enterprises and effectively monitor management behaviour. At the initial stage, it took the form of a contract between a subsidiary company and a ship under its control in which the latter took the responsibility of achieving certain end-results. This was, in turn, related to the economic interests of individuals on board the ship by rewards and penalties (Wan, 1988b).

In 1979, 'Yu Lin' and 'Lu Feng', managed by COSCO Guangzhou, implemented ECRS. The master and chief engineer of each ship chose officers and ratings, subject to consultation and with the approval of the personnel department ashore. Each ship entered into a three-year contract with the company for the responsibility of controlling the time and costs of ship repair and spares expenditure. These responsibilities were expressed in targets quantified by shore management and agreed by ship.

The rewards and penalties were set as the same proportion of the costs saved or overspent, although the percentage differed from item to item. For instance, if ship repair time was reduced by more than 10 days the ship could earn a reward of 15 per cent of the planned repair costs per day, calculated from the 11th day if the repair costs were saved, with 10 per cent of the saved costs being rewarded as bonus. One year later, the operating results of these two ships showed a significant improvement. The profit of 'Yu Lin' achieved 178.16 per cent of the planned amount, and 'Lu Feng' also made a profit, ending years of loss making.

The experiment with ECRS was then extended to cover 75 ships operated by COSCO Shanghai, Guangzhou, Dalian and Tianjin and the responsibilities were also extended to safety, service quality, time and quantity of ship repair, fuel costs, provisions, spares, voyage time and profit. By mid 1985, up to 269 of COSCO's ships of various types and sizes had adopted ECRS, accounting for 57 per cent of COSCO's ships. In

1988, the responsibilities held ashore were wholly transferred to the master of a ship and all COSCO's ships had implemented ECRS prior to 1990.

The implementation of ECRS over the years has greatly increased the efficiency of COSCO's shipping management. Firstly, there was, in general, a significant reduction in ship costs. Secondly, contract ships have reported better safety records whilst thirdly, shipboard management has been improved by increased team sense and job satisfaction, with crew on board found to be more disciplined, co-operative and responsible (Wan, 1988b). These improvements could be seen as resulting from a successful experiment of the theory of motivation on management (Weihrich and Koontz, 1994).

ECRS on Shore

In 1988, approved by the MOC, COSCO implemented ECRS within shore management. The ECRS took three forms: contracts between COSCO and MOC, contracts between COSCO and its subsidiaries, and contracts between a department and the company. Under the contract between COSCO and MOC, the development strategies were set to develop fleet management, focusing on container lines and expanding the companies' overseas business. COSCO was responsible for the control of safety, improvement of technology, earning profit and ensuring the transportation of important goods for the nation. The ECRS of the other two forms varied from company to company and the responsibility mainly covered the amount of profit, certain improvements in production technology and a growth in the company's real assets. The total wage bill of COSCO was linked to the achievement of the targets listed in the contract.

From 1988 to 1990, 90 per cent of COSCO's subsidiaries implemented ECRS, the volume of cargo transported increased by 4.5 per cent and the real assets of COSCO increased by 270 million US$. Since the COSCO Group's establishment in 1993 it has continuously implemented ECRS as a main strategy to improve management efficiency and to motivate management behaviour. ECRS has succeeded in raising productivity, profitability and investment and brought a substantial growth of diversified business. Nevertheless, several problems have been encountered in the implementation of ECRS. For example, there have been difficulties in setting up appropriate targets and there is evidence of short-sighted behaviour such as a reduced incentive to invest in new lines and exploitation of customers in the last year of the contract term as their immediate effects were not apparent.

Establishing Joint Ventures

Before 1979, there were only four shipping joint ventures in China established by the Chinese government, mainly with former socialist countries: Poland, Czechoslovakia, Albania and Tanzania. These joint ventures were in the fields of ship purchase and fleet management. Since the adoption of the open door policy and formulation of the policies to attract foreign investment in the late 1970s, the Chinese shipping industry has established numerous joint ventures with Japan, Holland, Singapore, and USA amongst others and their business has extended into ship repair, container manufacture, terminal construction and fleet operation. The main reasons for these foreign companies entering into joint ventures with China were to reduce their costs, enter new business areas, acquire new means of distribution and enter the domestic markets. The motives for the Chinese companies included acquisition of new technology, access to modern production and management techniques, and earning hard currency.

Motives for Joint Ventures

Whilst the foreign shipping companies attempted to increase their share of the Chinese market, COSCO also tried to obtain a share of the international market. Extending overseas business was set as a long-time development strategy since the Chinese government encouraged overseas investment and co-operation in 1979. Before COSCO began the restructuring of its overseas business in 1997, it had set up more than 50 joint ventures engaged in the fields of shipping agency, facility supply, chartering, ship repair, bunker supply, CY management and fleet management. The partners were mainly from developed countries such as the Netherlands, UK, Japan, and USA. The main reasons for this development were:

- The increasing joint venture experience in other industries in China. Thanks to a series of policies to attract foreign investment and co-operation, thousands of joint ventures were established in other industries such as electricity and manufacturing, from which COSCO has gained useful experience.

- The changing shipping environment. As the Chinese shipping market gradually opened up from 1979, COSCO's market share hovered around 20 per cent for trade to and from China by the mid 1980s. Expanding new markets were established as its main development strategy. In the 1980s COSCO established 20 joint ventures, which formed the basis of its overseas shipping service network.
- The improvement of diplomatic relationships between China and other countries. COSCO established the CO-Heung Shipping Company with Heung-A Shipping Co. of Korea in Seoul in March 1991, two years after the normalisation of diplomatic relations between China and South Korea. COSCO is the second Chinese shipping company to have entered the Korean market. The development of diplomatic relations between the two countries provided a good chance for COSCO to explore the Korean shipping market.
- To introduce advanced management technology. Through the operation of its joint ventures, concepts such as 'market and profit' and 'the free competition principle' were introduced to COSCO's joint ventures in the early 1980s, whilst their parent company was still operating under the planned system.

Benefits of Joint Ventures

Although there were many problems in managing the joint ventures (such as misunderstanding customs and differences in management style) the main benefits are that firstly, COSCO was able to become familiar with the foreign environment and management style quickly (Lee, Shen and Moon, 1996) secondly to share the risk with its foreign partner. Thirdly, it was able to expand its business into tourism, trade and freight forwarding into foreign countries – since 1994 it has begun to fine-tune its joint ventures abroad and change some of them into wholly owned companies. The years of partaking in joint ventures has provided good experience for COSCO to handle business with foreign partners and expand its overseas market.

Developing Container Lines

As the seventh biggest container line in the world in terms of slots deployed, COSCO has grown rapidly since launching its first service between Australia and China in 1978. In 1997, COSCO carried in excess of three million TEU. It currently owns 118 container vessels totalling about 210,000 TEU.

China started containerised transport in 1973, operated by COSCO, SINOTRANS and their Japanese partners. However, the Chinese fleet possessed only 12 x 200 TEU container ships and only 200 containers were manufactured in China by 1977. As a result, high value containerised general cargoes were mostly carried by Japanese carriers. In 1977, it was estimated that less than 5 per cent of containers were carried by the Chinese fleet.

In 1978, the containers shipped out of Shanghai increased to more than 700 TEU a month. In order to meet the explosive growth in the containerisation of Chinese trade, COSCO's fleet development strategy emphasised the necessity for container line development. In 1980 eight ro/ro's were built in Japan, their total capacity amounting to about 4,600 TEU. From 1982 to 1985 16 full container ships amounting to over 22,000 TEU were built and by the end of 1985, COSCO's full container fleet had reached 37, amounting to over 30,000 TEU. This had increased to about 85,000 TEU by the end of 1990 and in 1992 COSCO Shanghai took delivery of three 2,761 TEU full container ships with its container fleet by 1992 amounting to over 92,000 TEU.

Today, modernising its containership fleet continues to be a fundamental element of COSCO's liner strategy. However, during the 1980s and early 1990s tonnage for COSCO's services was acquired principally on the second-hand market. In 1993 the MOC tightened regulations on old ships and encouraged investment in newer tonnage (Zhang, 1997).

COSCO was confronted with a task of renewing and restructuring its fleet. Since COSCO Container Line's establishment in 1993 and 1997, it has taken delivery of eight 3,800 TEU ships and five 5,250 TEU post-Panamax units for its Europe/Asia and Asia/USWC services respectively. Six 5,250 TEU ships were deployed in 1999.

Moreover, it has upgraded several of its coastal services over this period, with new ships of between 300 TEU and 1,000 TEU capacity. The development of COSCO's container fleet is shown in Table 4.1.

Operational Alliance with Container Lines

In order to improve customer service, information technology and cost management, COSCO Container Lines merged with Shanghai Ocean Shipping Company in December 1997. All functions, including sales/marketing, fleet management and landside support services, have been concentrated in one company for the first time. The objectives of management were focused on cutting costs, enhancing service quality and responding more effectively to customer demands. In order to realise these objectives the new COSCO considered that co-operation with the top container lines in the world would be very important.

Table 4.1: The Development of COSCO Container Fleet (1978-97)

Year	Number	10,000 dwt	% Change	Capacity (TEU)	% Change
1978	2	1.64	-	-	-
1979	2	1.64	-	-	-
1980	1	0.71	-130.97	-	-
1981	2	1.64	56.70	-	-
1982	7	7.89	79.21	-	
1983	13	24.44	67.72	-	-
1984	22	36.41	32.88	-	-
1985	37	62.30	41.56	-	-
1986	42	70.71	11.89	35,387	-
1987	47	78.80	10.27	39,825	12.54
1988	61	101.34	22.24	51,065	28.22
1989	71	127.35	20.42	67,765	32.70
1990	85	159.31	20.06	84,994	25.42
1991	86	162.35	1.87	85,058	0.08
1992	92	173.86	6.62	92,556	8.82
1993	101	200.10	13.11	109,708	18.53
1994	120	267.17	25.10	158,635	44.60
1995	117	259.04	-3.14	154,048	-2.89
1996	116	263.69	1.76	157,242	2.07
1997	116	320.10	17.62	203,197	29.23

Source: Authors.

As the development of globalisation and M&A developed in other top container lines in the world, COSCO started its operation alliances in 1996 to further optimise the structure of its fleet and service route. In August 1996 it signed co-operation deals with K-Line and Yangming on the Europe/Asia, Transpacific and Europe/USEC trades. The co-operative arrangement has enabled the company to improve its sailing frequency in the core East/West trade offering three sailings a week between Europe/Asia as compared to one previously and it now provides access to six separate fixed-day weekly loops on the Asia/USWC route. Prior to the Transpacific tie up, COSCO offered its customers just two sailings a week off the West Coast.

With increasing competition on the home front, COSCO viewed the crosstrades sector as becoming very important to its future. In 1998 it entered into a slot purchase arrangement with Compania Sud Americanan de Vapores and commenced operations between northern Europe/Iberia and USA East Coast South (Fossey, 1998).

In May 1999, COSCO co-operated with Evergreen Marine Corporation Co. (Evergreen) on the Asia/South Africa and South American trades. This co-operation enabled COSCO to withdraw at least eight of its 2,000 TEU container ships from Asia/South Africa and South America lines in 1999 and re-deploy them to a new transpacific route predominantly serving northern China, including the ports of Dalian and Xingang.

More recently, COSCO Container Lines, Evergreen Marine Corp. Ltd., K-Line, and Malaysia International Shipping Corporation announced a new joint container service between South-western Asia (Sri Lanka and India) and Europe with effect from March 2001. The service offers weekly fixed-day service operated by six vessels ranging from 2,300 TEU to 2,700 TEU.

COSCO is not a party to any conference agreement. It is, however, a member of several other agreements. Following COSCO's signing up for the Intra-Asia Discussion Agreement in spring 1996, it joined the Westbound Transpacific Stabilisation Agreement in September 1997. Management now openly calls for more dialogue between conference and non-conference carriers. COSCO is also a member of The International Council of Containership Operators, The Israel Discussion Agreement, and the Transatlantic Bridge Agreement, which bridges FMC Agreements.

A more responsible attitude to pricing has been supported by a greater range of service offerings. COSCO is determined to move towards the standards set by carriers such as APL, Maersk, and the Japanese operators, and has over the past few years significantly expanded its value-added intermodal and reefer options. The new 5,250 TEU ships that it has phased into service since 1997, for instance, have 1,000 TEU of reefer space (Fossey, 1998).

Developing Multimodal Transportation

Since the concept of logistics was introduced to China in the early 1980s, quite a number of Chinese enterprises (some enterprises even use the word 'logistics' in their names) have expanded their business into logistical services. However, most of them only provide such conventional services as freight forwarding, warehousing and cargo transportation agency. None of them are able to provide a total transportation service package and, therefore, could not be considered as truly modern logistics enterprises.

In order to promote the modernisation of China's transport industry, the Chinese government has actively introduced experiences in logistics development from developed countries and boosted the growth of China's logistics industry. In 1997 and 1998, four foreign shipping companies were allowed to set up wholly owned logistics companies as an experimental measure. This is a tentative step towards the development of China's international logistics industry (Hu, 1999).

In order to extend its business into logistical services COSCO has been continuously developing multimodal transportation since the early 1990s. When the group was established in 1993, it formulated its overall strategy as '*down to the sea, on to the land and up to the sky*',[1] Based on this strategy, COSCO's multimodal transportation service has taken shape, with their container lines at its core, regional subsidiaries at home and abroad as its main bulk, and widespread on-site management, agency and outlet services as its pillar.

COSCO has developed a portfolio of multimodal transportation services offered to customers in China, aimed at satisfying their various transportation needs. The services range from 'base level services' to 'value-added services'. 'Base level service' means the basic services that a customer normally expects from a carrier, including trunk services and feeder services. 'Value added services' are those additional services that a customer does need but does not expect the carriers to offer without a special arrangement and additional cost.[2]

Base Level Services

The backbone of COSCO's base level services is its global network of trunk line services. Today, its trunk routes cover the major container trades between Asia and the Americas, and Asia and Europe, as well as the intra-Asia and Australia trades connecting main Chinese ports from north to south such as Dalian, Xingang, Qingdao, Shanghai, Xiamen and Hong Kong. Apart from direct calls at Chinese ports, COSCO is connected with every market on the globe. The liner services noted above are all well linked by a comprehensive global liner network, which expands COSCO's reach to more than 100 other ports all over the world.

For other coastal ports and ports on the major inland waterways, COSCO also operates feeder routes making timely connections with its trunk line vessels at the port of relay. The feeder routes include Dalian to Pusan, Yangtze River ports to Shanghai, Pearl River Delta ports to Shekou or Hong Kong feeder services.

Apart from the coastal and river ports, COSCO makes connections with inland cities via railway and road. Since it signed the 'Sea-rail Transportation Agreement' with the Ministry of Railway in 1988, it has begun to extend its business to rail container transportation. The sea-rail lines have increased from eight lines in 1996, to 32 in 2000, linking up major ports and cities such as Dalian-Harbin, Xingan-Xian and Shanghai-Chengdu. In March 2001, COSCO launched the Dalian-Changchun container train line, which was the first international container train line in the Northeast of China in co-operation with the railway department, the Port Authority of Dalian and COSCO Freight of Dalian.

Since the mid 1980s, COSCO has expanded its sea-road transportation. Its fleet of container tractors had increased to 1,290, with total slots of 2,346 TEU by 1997, about five times its 1985 level in terms of capacity, spreading not only through the main ports such as Guangzhou, Shanghai, Xiamen and Qingdao, but also to inland cities such as Kunming, Wuhan and Chengdo. In 1997, COSCO's road container transportation volume reached over 0.44 million TEU.

Value-added Services

In January 1998, COSCO Freight International Co. and its branches initiated the 'One Stop Service'[3] for customers, offering a range of value-added services. Having now developed considerable logistics capabilities they can design packages to suit the special needs of their customers. The value-added services include CFS stuffing, storage, customs clearance, order tracking and supply chain management.

After years of developing its multimodal transportation, COSCO now is working on a number of projects to extend its business into logistics in China in order to meet the increasing demand of customers. It will be forming a logistics company after organisational restructuring. Its target customer groups will be the trans-national companies with global supply chains. It will offer a total 'package' logistics service to them, supported by advanced information technology and its global logistics internet platform.

Building up the Information Network

In the shipping industry, the incorporation of the internet into business plans has become the key goal for businesses ranging from container lines to freight forwarders as the transportation industry converges toward the goal of logistics provision. Clients who want to deal with one company that can handle as much of the transportation chain as possible are driving rapid innovation (McElroy, 2000). 'Developing more dialogue with customers' became a key part of Maersk's overall strategy and GAMP has been implemented, giving Maersk's sales representatives an enormous competitive advantage.[4]

In China, COSCO was the first shipping company whose data flow passed EDI standards as early as 1990. It has realised a base platform for its e-commerce development. Since 1997 it has begun to push the development of e-commerce as part of its logistics development strategy.

The objectives of developing e-commerce in COSCO are, firstly, to increase the company's efficiency and enhance its competitive power and, secondly, to solve a series of practical problems such as blocked sales of products, ineffective information, hard capital turnover, commercial credit crisis and chain debt, that industrial and commercial enterprises encountered in market activities. The strategy of developing COSCO's e-commerce is aimed at customer's changing demands. Taking a global promotion system as its business platform, realignment of logistics, information flow and business process as its management platform and customer's satisfaction as its cultural and idea platform, COSCO is targeted to build e-transport and e-logistics systems based on the intellectual ability of the internet, 'soft' services and diversified forms of transport and to co-ordinate all this with environmental development.

Situation of E-commerce Development

COSCO finished the construction of its EDI centre and network between 1996 and 1997. The network has basically covered more than 50 large and medium sized domestic COSCO Freight and PENAVICO offices. It has realised its interconnection with GEIS EDI Centre through the EDI Centre in Beijing and connected COSCO companies overseas. At present, COSCO has realised the EDI transfer of data of transportation manifest, cargo plan and container management, thus entering the forefront of domestic transport industry in the field of e-commerce.

In 1997, COSCO invested considerable funds and manpower building a COSCO Net for global communications. By October 1999, COSCO had formed an e-mail network covering China, Singapore, Japan, America, Europe and Australia, with Beijing as its centre, enabling COSCO's staff to conduct their daily business through e-mail.

In January 1997, COSCO formally opened its website [www.cosco.com.cn]. Its subsidiaries such as COSCON, COSBULK and COSCO Guangzhou were built up consecutively. In September 1998 COSCO Container Lines was the first corporation in China to provide sailing schedule bulletins and booking service online. The introduction of online service system overcame the problems of low speed and efficiency, big work loads and the high rate of errors that appeared in the traditional service. It has brought freight forwarding directly to the customer's desk so that with their PC's they are in control of all the business formalities of consignment booking, document production and information inquiry that are needed in cargo exporting.

The establishment of COSCO's websites has greatly accelerated information circulation between it and its customers. It has improved efficiency. In March 2000 the 'COSCO Network' was established in the Cayman Islands to strengthen its ability to harness the latest technology and to create a business to business network that would manage the entire logistic chain. Right after the acquisition of this Network by COSCO International in September 2000, it has continuously input other logistics-related capital into COSCO International as an initiative designed to transfer the company into an online logistics network service and internet telecommunication service provider. An objective of COSCO is to get into the Blue Index and to be a major online logistics company. COSCO International is currently discussing with some domestic and overseas network companies for the planned acquisition of other e-commerce platform companies.

Conclusion

COSCO's development strategy was made possible by the Chinese government's economic reform and its 'open door' policy. The ECRS was then implemented on COSCO's ships after its successful application in Chinese agricultural reform and these contractual targets provided greater efficiency as job satisfaction, discipline and co-operative responsibility improved with motivated management. ECRS was then applied to COSCO's on shore management at the time it was being introduced to SOEs throughout China. The freedom and motivation given to former SOEs since the Chinese government's adoption of the open door policy in late 1970s has permitted and driven COSCO to establish numerous joint ventures with overseas shipping firms. A result of these unions is that much has been learned and technology and strategy have been acquired as well as an overall understanding of global markets seen from a new perspective. Having separated from the MOC and emerging into a strong, independent shipping company, COSCO continuously adjusts its development strategy, focusing on the developing container lines, extending into the logistic business and building up an information network enabling it to metamorphose into a global carrier.

This century will see a ten-year development plan detailing broad aims including the need to embrace greater market orientation, the strengthening of shipping operations, the development of a comprehensive logistics programme and optimised land activities in order to achieve sustainable group development (Fairplay, 2000). The main challenges facing COSCO in the future are how to convert itself from a global carrier to a global logistics operator and how moving on from a multinational operation to a multinational company will be achieved. Needless to say, how to strengthen its market competitiveness will continue to be the driving force that COSCO has become known for.

Notes

[1] While maintaining shipping as the core of the business, COSCO extended its business activities into land based businesses and air transport, including those ancillary activities of the core business such as road haulage, seaports, warehouse, railway transport, information network and so on.

[2] As customer expectation changes, the designation of each logistics service changes also. A value-added service of today may become a base level product if most carriers offer it without charging additional cost.

[3] The freight forwarding companies of COSCO will be responsible for all the

services that their customers are entitled to receive from the first step of space booking, arrangement of empty container pickup to customs declaration, quarantine and commodity inspections, amendments of documents, until the final steps of issuing B/L and invoices, collection of check list and drawbacks.

[4] http://www.broden.com/maersk-sealand.html.

5 Port Competition and Co-operation in Hong Kong and South China

Dong-Wook Song
Department of Shipping and Transport Logistics
The Hong Kong Polytechnic University, Hong Kong

Introduction

The economy of Hong Kong, as the entrepôt to the Chinese mainland, has enjoyed a high growth rate over the last few decades. When Hong Kong developed its container ports in order to accommodate the regional economic boom, its counterparts in China were left far behind and there was no serious port competition from China. As China develops its economy however, the port of Hong Kong faces real challenges from Chinese ports, particularly from southern ones. Interestingly, the hand-over of its sovereignty to China in 1997 caused an issue of competition and co-operation between these ports. This paper aims to describe the possible competition and co-operation of the adjacent container ports in Hong Kong and South China.

The fact that the global economy is shifting towards the newly industrialising countries in Asia and that greater sea-borne trade links exist between Asian nations, is resulting in rapid, regional, economic development and growth. Since international trade is carried predominantly by sea transport, major container ports play a crucial role in regional economies. The latest available statistics show that, in terms of annual container throughputs, five Asian ports are ranked among the top ten in the world, including the top four – Hong Kong, Singapore, Kaohsiung and Pusan – as presented in Table 5.1.

Table 5.1: Container Port Traffic League (TEU p.a.)

	Container Port	1999	1998	Country
1	Hong Kong	16,210,000	14,580,000	China
2	Singapore	15,944,800	15,135,600	Singapore
3	Kaohsiung	6,985,361	6,271,053	Taiwan
4	Pusan	6,439,589	5,752,955	Korea
5	Rotterdam	6,343,020	6,011,526	Netherlands
6	Long Beach	4,408,480	4,097,689	USA
7	Shanghai	4,206,000	3,100,000	China
8	Los Angeles	3,828,851	3,378,219	USA
9	Hamburg	3,740,000	3,550,000	Germany
10	Antwerp	3,614,246	3,265,750	Belgium

Source: Port Development International (2000).

Amongst Asian economies, the Chinese economy is arguably regarded as the world's most fascinating in the modern era. As the entrepôt to the Chinese mainland, the economy of Hong Kong has enjoyed a high rate of economic development until the Asian financial turmoil that broke out at the end of 1997. When the Hong Kong economy commenced its dramatic economic growth with the other 'tiger economies' and developed its container ports in order to accommodate the regional container traffic accordingly, its counterparts in China were left far behind. Consequently, there has been no serious port competition from the Chinese mainland in the last twenty years and the role of Hong Kong ports as a regional hub has been aggrandised.

However, since China has been developing its economy at a two digit growth rate since the early 1990s, the port of Hong Kong faces real challenges from ports on the Chinese mainland, in particular from those in the south such as Chiwan, Shekou and Yantian. Furthermore, the historical hand-over of sovereignty to China in the middle of 1997 caused the issue of competition and co-operation between the ports to be more momentous. Even after the hand-over in mid-1997, when Hong Kong became officially a part of China, Hong Kong still remains an independent customs territory according to the Basic Law. This unique situation is obviously an interesting and important area for investigation.

With this background in mind, this paper aims to review the current and prospective status of those ports and to describe the possible competition and co-operation of the adjacent container ports in Hong Kong and South China from a strategic perspective.

Trade Patterns Between Hong Kong and South China

Since sea transport is derived from international trade, it is logical to examine the trade patterns between the two regions before moving on to the main theme. Hong Kong has always been open to China, and Hong Kong businessmen currently receive no special treatment from the Chinese mainland compared to other foreign business people. Due to geographical proximity, extended family relationships and linguistic closeness, however, Hong Kong businesses often get informal extra incentives, particularly from local authorities in Guangdong (Fung, 1996).

The strategic location, the modern facilities in banking, finance and insurance systems and the modern telecommunication and transportation network of Hong Kong all facilitate the city as the Chinese mainland's main gateway to the rest of the world. On the other hand, to a large extent, the world continues to view Hong Kong as the main entrance to the Chinese mainland (Sung, 1998). A large volume of trade in both countries is the so-called entrepôt trade. In other words, the role of Hong Kong in China's trade is by and large as an intermediary. In this respect, two notable trade patterns between the Chinese mainland and Hong Kong are worth discussing: that is, re-exports and outward processing.

Re-Exports Trade Pattern

Over the last few years, the Chinese mainland has been the largest market for Hong Kong's total exports, followed by the United States, Japan, Taiwan and Singapore. Domestic exports from Hong Kong to the Chinese mainland were HK$ 314,651 million in 1998, up 6.3 per cent compared to the previous year in terms of real value, which is shown in Table 5.2. On the import trade, the Chinese mainland also remained the most important partner of Hong Kong imports, accounting for approximately 38 per cent of their total value in 1998.

Re-exports take place when imports to Hong Kong are consigned to a buyer in Hong Kong, who takes legal possession of these cargoes. Re-exports are also required to clear customs. The buyer in Hong Kong carries out a value-added economic activity, then re-exports the goods elsewhere. The value-added activity may include grading, packaging, bottling, assembling, and types of minor manufacturing functions which do not, however, change the basic nature of the goods. Hong Kong origin is not therefore, supposed to be conferred by the Hong Kong government body. If the process alters substantially the nature of the products, then the goods are entitled to be named as goods 'made in Hong Kong'. Exports of goods 'made in Hong Kong' are classified as domestic exports rather than as re-exports (Sung, 1991).

Table 5.2: Hong Kong's Top 5 Trading Partners (1998, million HK$)

	Major Partners	Total Trade		Total exports		Re-Exports	
		Value	%	Value	%	Value	%
1	China	1,116,117	36.3	314,651	35.2	276,012	35.9
2	USA	441,826	14.4	205,968	23.0	170,099	22.1
3	Japan	310,011	10.1	46,756	5.2	42,224	5.5
4	Taiwan	161,158	5.2	22,658	2.5	18,350	2.4
5	Singapore	116,975	3.8	19,730	2.2	16,190	2.1

Source: Census and Statistics Department (1999).

Overall, re-exports via Hong Kong have registered a significant growth in recent years. In 1998 alone, the value of re-exports to all markets was HK$ 718,631 million, which is more than 18 per cent higher than in the previous year. In general, the value of re-exports has been growing rapidly and become a more and more important wealth creating trade pattern to the Hong Kong economy, while the value of domestic exports has been shrinking. In 1998, re-exports accounted for 83 per cent, up from 79 per cent in 1997 and from 75 per cent in 1996. The Chinese mainland is the most crucial source of goods re-exported through the Hong Kong border: Chinese goods re-exported via the territory of Hong Kong amounted to HK$ 276,012 million, which was more than a third of total re-exports handled in 1998.

Outward Processing Trade Pattern

Outward processing arrangements are made if companies subcontract all or part of their production processes. These trading patterns often occur between Hong Kong companies and manufacturing entities in China. Raw materials or semi-manufactures are exported to China for further processing. The Chinese mainland entities engaged can be local enterprises, joint ventures or some other form of business involving foreign investment (Hong Kong Government, 1994). About four-fifths of Hong Kong manufacturers have transferred production to China, and 25,000 factories in the Pearl River Delta (PRD) region of Guangdong are engaged in outward processing for Hong Kong companies (Hong Kong Government, 1995).

Table 5.3 shows the extent of domestic exports and imports associated with Hong Kong processing in the Chinese mainland, which shows an ever-increasing trend.

Table 5.3: Domestic Exports and Imports Concerning Outward Processing (%)

Year	Hong Kong Exports to China	Hong Kong Imports from China
1990	79.0	61.8
1991	76.5	67.6
1992	74.3	72.1
1993	74.0	73.8
1994	71.4	75.9
1995	71.4	74.4
1996	72.8	74.9
1997	75.6	75.2
1998	76.8	76.6

Note: Figures indicate per cent of total Hong Kong domestic exports to and imports from China.
Source: Census and Statistics Department (1999).

In summary, both re-exports and outward-processing business activities are substantial characteristics of the trade between Hong Kong and the Chinese mainland. It is moreover speculated that Hong Kong's trade pattern with China will continue to grow. Given its geographical location and its know-how in banking and finance, insurance and telecommunication and transportation, Hong Kong is expected to continue to serve as the gateway to and from the Chinese mainland, which benefits each side via trade, so as to create and sustain economic synergy in the region.

The Container Ports in Hong Kong and South China

Seaborne Container Cargo Traffic

The port of Hong Kong has been the world's busiest container port for the last decade, with remarkable TEU throughputs as shown in Figure 5.1. An exception was the year 1998, when the number one position was taken over by the port of Singapore (Lloyd's List Maritime Asia, 1999). This was due partly to Singapore's major efforts to become a hub port in the region, and partly to the southern Chinese ports' efforts to penetrate the regional market, with a significant average growth rate of over 10 per cent over the past few years.

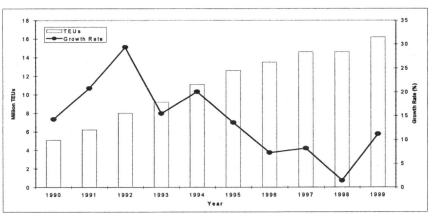

Source: Containerisation International Yearbook (1999).

Figure 5.1: Container Traffic in the Port of Hong Kong

Historically, Hong Kong's port has expanded along with the rapid economic development in Southeast Asian countries and China and greater international trade connections between these areas and the rest of the world. Rimmer (1996) points out the role of Hong Kong in global as well as regional container transport and views Hong Kong as a regional hub port or load centre, which cannot be separated from the regional hub in Southeast Asia and South China. Today Hong Kong's port however, faces more severe competitive circumstances, particularly the challenges from regional ports such as Singapore and Yantian, located in southern China. This problem is well documented recently: for example, Wong and Beresford (1996a), Bangsberg (1998), Wong (1999), and Mooney (2000).

As a consequence, Hong Kong's position as a leading load and transhipment centre for China-bound cargoes is under threat from a number of developments. These include its reversion to China in 1997, port development in China itself, speculation on the opening of direct shipping links between Taiwan and the Chinese mainland and the easing of restrictions on access to Chinese ports for foreign shipping lines (Drewry Shipping Consultants, 1995). To make the situation worse, Hong Kong faces congestion problems at its ports which distract from its competitiveness.

Almost every major international container shipping company is now engaged in trade with China and operates direct line services to an increasing number of Chinese ports. The occurrence of the direct services by major lines has only been within the last few years. In the past, the large proportion of container trade with China was transhipped via Hong Kong, Taiwan and Korea. In spite of the fact that a significant amount of container trade bound for China is still transhipped through these three countries, mainly Hong Kong, the Chinese government is operating a deliberate policy to reduce the ratio (Drewry Shipping Consultants, 1999). Table 5.4 shows the steady but sharply increasing proportion of direct callings by major container shipping companies at Chinese ports, with the portion at Hong Kong's port becoming relatively less significant.

Table 5.4: Direct Calls to Chinese Ports (1990 to 1998) (number of lines calling)

	1990	1991	1992	1993	1994	1995	1996	1997	1998
Shanghai	4	19	13	13	13	17	15	20	19
Tianjin	8	19	18	18	18	18	18	18	18
Dalian	3	12	11	11	9	9	10	10	10
Qingdao	6	9	9	9	9	11	10	10	10
Yantian	0	0	0	0	0	1	1	6	9
Shekou	0	0	0	0	0	3	3	7	6
Chiwan	0	0	0	0	0	1	1	1	4
Others	7	10	11	12	12	18	16	14	15
Total	28	69	62	63	61	78	74	86	91
Hong Kong	55	46	48	48	45	44	39	47	47

Source: Drewry Shipping Consultants (1999, p. 63).

Table 5.4 shows that the number of direct callings at the three South Chinese ports – Yantian, Shekou and Chiwan – has escalated, particularly since the handover in 1997: 19 lines calling directly to those container ports in 1998 compared with 14 in 1997 and only five in 1996, respectively. Table 5.5 shows the details of the direct ocean container services offered by Yantian, Shekou and Chiwan. As shown in Tables 5.4 and 5.5, among the three promising ports, Yantian is largely considered as the front runner against its Hong Kong counterpart, through attracting many major international shipping lines to use its services for Trans-Pacific and Euro-Asia routes. Yantian also provides frequent feeder services to Hong Kong and other major Chinese coastal ports.

Table 5.5: Shipping Companies Calling at Shenzhen Ports

	Route	Frequency	Shipping Line	Ship Slots (TEU)	Commencing Time
Yantian	North America	Once a week	Maersk/ Sea-Land	3,932-6,000	March 1995
	North America	Once a week	New Global Alliance	4,800	January 1996
	North America	Once a week	New Global Alliance	4,300	January 1996
	North America	Once a week	K-line	3,720	March 1998
	North America	Once a week	Grand Alliance	4,830	February 1998
	North America	Once a week	Grand Alliance	2,900-3,600	February 1998
	Europe	Once a week	Maersk/ Sea-Land	2,959-4,300	July 1994
	Europe	Once a week	New Global Alliance	3,980	January 1996
	Europe	Once a week	Grand Alliance	4,600	February 1998
	Australia	Once a week	Far East Transport-ation (HK) Limited	1,274	July 1998
	North America	Once a week	Evergreen	5,346	October 1998
	Europe	Once a week	CMA	3,501	June 1998
Shekou	Europe	Once a week	Grand Alliance	4,000	June 1996
	North America	Once a week	Zim	3,500	July 1997
	North America	Once a week	COSCO	5,250	October 1997
	Europe	Once a week	Zim	3,500	February 1998
	Australia	Once a week	P&O N/ OOCL/Zim	2,300	May 1998
Chiwan	Europe	Once a week	North EuroAsia/ Medi-terranean	3,066	May 1996
	Australia	Once a week	Medi-terranean	1,100	August 1997

Source: Ministry of Transport (1998).

Yantian is located in the eastern part of the Shenzhen Special Economic Zone, which is one of the major economic powerhouses in China. The port of Yantian commenced its operation in 1994 and currently has Maersk/Sealand, COSCO and the members of Global Alliance calling. Using the current facilities, the port handled 1.59 million TEUs in 1999 alone, 54 per cent up relative to the figures for 1998. The port capacity will be up to 1.7 million TEUs with the completion of the planned Phase Two development scheme. According to the long-term plan set up by the Chinese government, up to four ship berths can be constructed in the future (Shippers Today, 1997). It has also been developing into a well-organised port with international connections.

Moreover, the geographical condition of the port of Yantian puts an additional strength to its potential to be a major competitor against the port of Hong Kong. The speed of Yantian's potential development, however, depends largely on the pace of cargo expansion created in the surrounding region. To generate more cargo flow, Yantian International Container Terminals has connected itself to Hong Kong and coastal cities in northern Guangdong and Fujian Provinces by feeder services to supplement its natural cargo base in Shenzhen and the adjacent areas. It is expected that many Chinese cities will be linked to Yantian through a connecting line of the Beijing-Kowloon Railway. These overall features imply that the port of Yantian has the highest potential among southern Chinese ports to develop itself into a major container port in the near future.

Administrative and Ownership Structures

Hong Kong

The administrative and ownership structure of Hong Kong's container terminals can be depicted as a three-tiered hierarchy. Since it maintains ownership over the land upon which the container terminals are built, the Government of the Hong Kong Special Administrative Region (HKSAR) constitutes the highest tier in the administrative structure. Under the HKSAR Government, the Marine Department acts in the capacity of port authority and deals with all navigational matters of the regional port. It has responsibility for vessel traffic management, the safety standards of all classes and types of vessels and other regulatory matters and is involved in the strategic planning of port developments. The Hong Kong Port and Maritime Board is also involved in the planning of new port developments, but itself is not a governmental body. Rather, it comprises representatives of Hong Kong's private sector shipping and port interests as well as from government. It is constituted as an advisory body to the HKSAR Government.

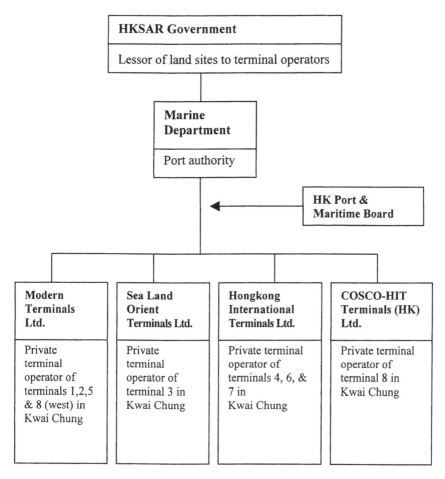

Source: Cullinane and Song (2001).

Figure 5.2: Administrative and Ownership Structure of Hong Kong Ports

The HKSAR Government is the lessor of land sites to the private terminal operating companies. Neither the Government nor the Marine

Department owns or operates container terminal facilities. These are all privately owned and operated by four private companies: Modern Terminals Limited (MTL), Sea-Land Orient Terminals Limited (hereafter referred to as 'SLOT'), Hong Kong International Terminals Limited (HIT) and COSCO-HIT Terminals (HK) Limited (hereafter referred to as 'COSCO-HIT'). The overall administrative structure of the container port of Hong Kong is illustrated in Figure 5.2.

MTL has provided services since September 1972, with terminals 1, 2 and 5 and two berths at terminal 8 (west). MTL will be offering a new facility at terminal 9 (south) with a 1,210m quay and a throughput capacity of 4.45 million TEU when the on-going construction is completed. SLOT is the operator of terminal 3 in the Kwai Chung Container Terminal. The company was established in 1981 to develop a comprehensive cargo handling and distribution facility as a dedicated terminal within the port of Hong Kong. In January 1987, it opened Asia's largest container freight station at berth 3 of Hong Kong's Kwai Chung Container Terminal. HIT, a member of the Hutchison Port Holdings Group, was set up in 1969 and now operates container terminals 4, 6 and 7. In 1996, HIT was offered the right to develop and operate two berths in container terminal 9. COSCO-HIT was formed in 1991 by the joint venture of HIT and China Ocean Shipping Company (COSCO) and is currently the terminal operator of terminal 8 (East) in Kwai Chung.

South China: Shenzhen

The administrative and ownership structure of Shenzhen port is shown in Figure 5.3. The port of Yantian is operated by Yantian International Container Terminals Limited (hereafter referred to as 'YICT'), established in 1993, which is a joint venture between the Hutchison Ports Yantian Limited (73 per cent), a subsidiary of the Hutchison Port Holdings Group, and the Shenzhen Yantian Port Group (27 per cent). YICT is equipped with advanced port facilities and is well served by inland transport links.

Shekou port lies on the east bank of the Pearl River. Similar to Yantian, it is well positioned geographically to take advantage of business flowing to and from the Pearl River estuary. Its development potential will be enhanced by the opening of the Tonggu Waterway. The container terminal is owned by Shekou Container Terminal Limited, opened in 1991, which is a joint venture between China Merchants (SCT) Holdings, P&O Ports, Swire Pacific and COSCO. The terminal has been jointly managed by P&O Ports and Modern Terminals Limited from May 1998.

Chiwan is a relatively small port when compared to Yantian and Shekou. With its continuous development in container handling facilities, it can act as a sub-distribution centre for the container business in Hong Kong. The terminal operator is the Shenzhen Chiwan Kaifeng Container Terminal Company, which has joint investments from Chiwan Wharf Holdings Limited (55 per cent), Kerry Holdings (HK) Limited (25 per cent), China Merchants Holding (International) Company and Modern Terminals Limited (20 per cent).

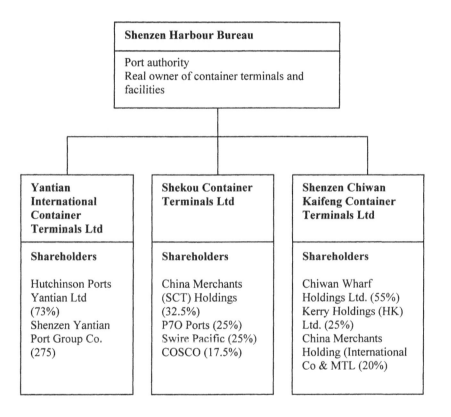

Source: Cullinane and Song (2001).

Figure 5.3: Administrative and Ownership Structure of Shenzhen Ports

Inter-relationship

Based on a review of each port's organisational structures, it is found that the ports in the region are competing against each other, but at the same time, they are working in a co-operative form for mutual benefits. The inter-relationship between the ports can be simplified by the illustration of Figure 5.4 in terms of their inter and intra competition and co-operation.

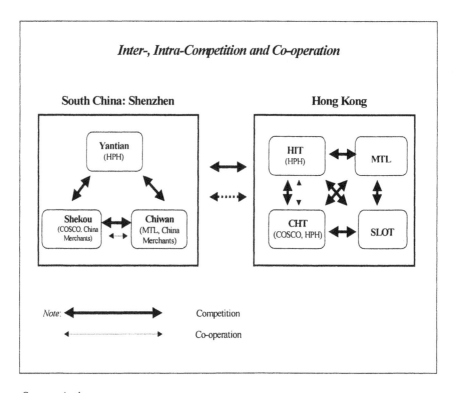

Source: Author.

Figure 5.4: Inter-relationship between Hong Kong and South China Ports

On the Hong Kong side, HIT, MTL, COSCO-HIT and SLOT compete against each other for container operations within Hong Kong territory. However, only HIT and MTL are in real competition, since SLOT is a dedicated terminal for its mother liner company Sea Land (before the merger with Maersk); COSCO-HIT mainly deals with COSCO's cargoes.

More importantly, COSCO-HIT and HIT have the Hutchison Port Holdings Group as their common owner, which means, for the sake of its interests, that co-operation is facilitated in order to combat the other two players in the market.

On the other side, in Shenzhen, local competition exists between the three ports: Yantian, Shekou and Chiwan. Due to the port ownership pattern, competition is especially keen between Yantian and the other two ports. There may be some form of co-operation between Shekou and Chiwan through the common ownership of the China Merchants Holding (International) Company. This can be further supported by the fact that MTL, one of the shareholders of Chiwan port, was awarded the management contract for Shekou Container Terminals when it extended its operations to the Chinese mainland in May 1998.

Today the Hong Kong operators have control, to some extent, of the operation of key ports in South China through a variety of co-operative measures such as joint ventures. This phenomenon intensifies and extends the competition between the container port operators from local competition to regional competition, while greatly enhancing the co-operation between the port of Hong Kong and its counterparts in South China. The two major players in Hong Kong, the Hutchison Port Holdings Group and MTL, are also involved to a great extent in Yantian and Chiwan respectively. The two companies compete locally within Hong Kong and Shenzhen, and also regionally between the ports of Hong Kong and Shenzhen.

In spite of such fierce competition, there also exists some form of co-operation between these ports. As shown in Figure 5.4, the Hutchison Port Holdings Group is particularly active in the private sector in Chinese ports. Co-operation exists between Hong Kong and Yantian through the Hutchison Port Holdings Group's common ownership. Co-operation exists between Hong Kong and Shekou through COSCO's common ownership. Co-operation exists between Hong Kong and Chiwan through MTL's common ownership.

Port Co-Opetition?

In this respect, Hong Kong and South China should take into serious consideration a new strategic approach – '*co-opetition*', a term coined by Brandenburger and Nalebuff (1996). The term 'co-opetition' is a mixture of competition and co-operation, thus having a strategic implication that those engaged in the same or similar market should 'collaborate to compete' as a win-win strategy, rather than a win-lose one. If business is regarded as a game, who are the players and what are their roles in the market? There are several parties involved in the market: customers and suppliers. Business cannot be carried out without them. As a result, naturally, there exist competitors. However, there is one more important group which is often overlooked but equally important – those who provide complementary rather than competing services. Brandenburger and Nalebuff (1996) name this group as 'complementors', a counterpart to the term 'competitors'. This relatively new concept stems from an idea initiated by Jorde and Teece (1989, p. 25), who note that:

> whereas co-operation among firms was once a subject confined to anti-trust case books, it is increasingly a topic for discussion . . . Indeed, ways in which firms can *co-operate to compete* are receiving considerable attention . . . .

This argument is in line with the current phenomenon in the liner shipping industry, which can be characterised by a movement towards strategic alliances between major international companies. In fact, Juhel (2000) initiates a co-operative concept between ports in order for them to adapt themselves to a flexible traffic distribution pattern through several port outlets. Again, Avery (2000) proposes strategic alliances between adjacent container ports – *'port strategic alliances'* – as a counter-strategic option in order to survive the ever-increasing competitive business environment.

In simple terms, port competition refers to commercial port rivalries and to the competitive efforts these rivalries induce (Fleming, 1997). South China needs additional ports; these ports will stimulate economic growth, which is good for the Chinese economy and, to some extent, good for Hong Kong as well. The additional container traffic in this area will increase the opportunity for additional shipping calls at Hong Kong and enhance maritime support services. Wong and Beresford (1996b) stress that any additional spur to competition can be good for Hong Kong – more competition will improve the standard of services provided.

Relative to the port of Hong Kong, however, Yantian port enjoys two major advantages for cargoes originating in or bound for South China (Cheng and Wong, 1997):

- Shorter trucking time due to not having to cross the Shenzhen-Hong Kong border; and
- Lower tariffs – the factory-to-ship costs incurred by shippers are lower when using these ports than when using the port of Hong Kong.

The relative advantages outlined above are even enforced by recent transportation trends in the regions in terms of route choices of cargoes. The port of Yantian has, however, an equal disadvantage in that much of the region's industrial output is created in the western PRD region. The Port Development Board (1995) points out that, as Hong Kong is well connected with the PRD by river, and Yantian is not, the river trade represents a major advantage to Hong Kong in competition with Yantian. The growth of river transport between the two areas continues to experience marginal increases.

At present however, port planning in Hong Kong cannot be implemented without taking into account Chinese issues (Tupper, 1998). While Hong Kong tries to remain the global and regional hub port for South China in the future, it is also important that Hong Kong recognise the importance of regular contacts and co-operation with the Shenzhen Port Authority through information exchange on port development strategies, and understand what facilities are required to optimally provide for the needs of its customers in the region.

Table 5.6: A Framework of TDS Options for Ports

	Scenario A		Scenario B
	I (*Steady Growth*)	**II (*High Growth*)**	**(*Extra High Growth*)**
Ports	• Container hub ports at Hong Kong and Yantian • Bulk cargo port at Yantian • Feeder ports at Shekou, Macau, Zhuhai and Pearl River towns	• Container hub port at Hong Kong • Bulk cargo port at Yantian • Feeder ports at Shekou, Macau, Zhuhai and Pearl River towns	• Container hub ports at Hong Kong, Yantian, and Gaolan • Bulk cargo ports at Yantian and Gaolan • Feeder ports at Shekou, Macau, Zhuhai and Pearl River towns

Source: Extracted from Fung (1995, pp. 301-302).

Turning to the area in question, Fung (1995) establishes a long-term strategic plan called the 'Territorial Development Strategy (TDS)' using a scenario approach. Table 5.6 shows a framework applicable to the port industry in Hong Kong and South China under this scenario.

With economic trends and visions, Table 5.6 indicates two development scenarios postulated for the formulation of the TDS development options. *Scenario A* assumes the PRD region as Hong Kong's primary economic hinterland. Two sub-scenarios have been developed under *Scenario A*: that is, steady growth and high growth. On the other hand, *Scenario B* includes both the PRD and the inner provinces in China as the economic hinterland.

Scenario AI assumes a partnership relationship between Hong Kong and the PRD in their development, Hong Kong retaining its traditional role as an entrepôt but is likely to experience a slower rate of growth. Higher growth under *Scenario A (AII)* assumes that Hong Kong will be the primary centre of development of the PRD, being the key trading outlet, service and financing centre for the region. Finally, extra high growth under *Scenario B* assumes that Hong Kong's influence will reach the inner provinces of China. These two scenarios are not mutually exclusive. *Scenario B* can be regarded as the long-term logical extension of *Scenario A*.

It can be said that the current economic situation in the area falls into *Scenario AI* – a slow and steady recovery period out of the financial crisis. Hence, a form of partnership or collaboration between the two parties is likely to be inevitable.

Conclusions

This paper can be concluded by stating the rationales for the current and prospective collaborating pattern within the container ports of the region. In general, organisations that involve co-operation can achieve at least more-or-less overlapping objectives, which are risk reduction, economies of scale, rationalisation, technology exchanges, co-opting or blocking competition, overcoming government-mandated trade or investment barriers, facilitating the initial international expansion of inexperienced firms and vertical quasi-integrated advantages of linking the complementary contributions of the partners in a value chain (Contractor and Lorange, 1988). The objective of co-opting or blocking competition is particularly true for the current situation of the container ports in Hong Kong and South China. Potential competition can be co-opted by forming a strategic alliance with the competitor, a way of 'collaborating to compete' (i.e. *co-opetition*). Furthermore, a co-opetitive alliance can strengthen both partners against outsiders even as it may weaken one partner against the other (Hamel *et al.*, 1989).

The Hutchison Port Holdings Group realises that the port of Yantian is a major competitor against the port of Hong Kong. In order to avoid the severe rivalry between the ports, the Hutchison Port Holdings Group decided to invest in Yantian for collaboration. The ports can co-operate in a win-win strategy against outsiders, like MTL, rather than compete against each other in a win-lose strategy. MTL also realises that the South Chinese port is threatening the competitiveness of the port of Hong Kong. Consequently, MTL has invested in Chiwan and gained the management contract for Shekou in order to form co-opetitive alliances and block the competition. More importantly for MTL, the Hutchison Port Holdings Group has strengthened its market power through collaboration. In order to compete with the Hutchison Port Holdings Group, MTL must also strengthen its market power through some effective means.

A recent report (China Ports, 1999) estimates that less than 20 per cent of China's cargoes are containerised, compared with the global average of 45-50 per cent, which reflects, on the one hand, the potential for the growth of containerised cargoes in China and, on the other, the bottleneck of infrastructure for container transportation. Moreover, the demand for container transportation will increase tremendously after China's entry into the WTO; the co-operative strategies between the ports of Hong Kong and South China will be extremely crucial in facing all these challenges.

Given the aforementioned discussion, it can be concluded that, as a result of the rapid integration between Hong Kong and South China in the last decade, a structural transformation has already unfolded in the territory's economy. The mutual benefits have been enormous, but negative problems are equally visible. Therefore, important challenges lie ahead.

As far as the port industry is concerned, Hong Kong is at the moment handling a very large share of China's external trade – the 'China factor' is undoubtedly the major driving force for the further development of the Hong Kong economy. China, however, is catching up fast as it begins the development of the economy's infrastructure, including its port facilities.

The main concern is not the resulting form of the integrated port system, but the process of its formation. The possible evolution of the regional container transport system can be regarded as a logistics approach (Wang, 1997) which focuses on the importance of 'soft integration' rather than hardware consolidation. Hong Kong people should focus on getting the best out of combining the territory's expertise with the huge market and resources of the Chinese mainland.

Acknowledgments

All the port operators who made contributions to this work are gratefully acknowledged. The author also thankfully acknowledges the Hong Kong Polytechnic University Grant (G-T172) for the financial support which has allowed the further development of this line of research.

References

Avery, P. (2000) *Strategies for Container Ports*, A Cargo Systems Report, IIR Publication Limited, London.

Bangsberg, P. T. (1998) Hong Kong Container Volume Growth Slowed by Diversion to China, *Journal of Commerce*, July 20th.

Brandenburger, A. M. and Nalebuff, B. J. (1996) *Co-opetition*, A Currency Book, New York.

Census and Statistics Department (1999) *Hong Kong Trade Statistics*, Hong Kong.

Cheng, L. K. and Wong, Y. C. (1997) *Port Facilities and Container Handling Services*, City University of Hong Kong Press, Hong Kong.

Containerisation International Yearbook (1999) Emap Business Communications Limited, London.

China Ports (1999) China's Ports and Terminals, 19 October, p. 10.

Contractor, F. and Lorange, P. (1988) Why Should Firms Co-operate? – The Strategy and Economics Basis for Co-operative Ventures, in Contractor, F. and Lorange, P. (eds), *Co-operative Strategies in International Business*, Lexington Books, New York, pp. 3-30.

Cullinane, K. and Song, D-W. (2001) Administrative and Ownership Structure of Asian Container Ports, *International Journal of Maritime Economics*, 3, 2, 175-197.

Drewry Shipping Consultants (1999) *China: Opportunities and Challenges for World shipping*, London.

Fleming, D. K. (1997) The Meaning of Port Competition, *Proceedings of International Conference of the International Association of Maritime Economist (IAME)*, London, 22-24 September.

Fung, C. K. (1995) Hong Kong's Territorial Development Strategy, in Yeh, G. O. and Mak, C. K. (eds.), *Chinese Cities and China's Development: a Preview of the Future Role of Hong Kong*, Centre of Urban Planning and Environmental Management, University of Hong Kong, Hong Kong, 295-309.

Fung, K. C. (1996) Mainland Chinese Investment in Hong Kong: How Much, Why and So What? *Journal of Asian Business*, 12, 2, 21-39.

Hamel, G., Doz, Y. and Prahalad, C. (1989) Collaborate With Your Competitors – and Win, *Harvard Business Review*, Jan-Feb, 133-139.

Hong Kong Government (1994) *First Quarter Economic Report 1994*, Hong Kong.

Hong Kong Government (1995) *Economic Background*, Hong Kong.

Jorde, T. M. and Teece, D. J. (1989) Competition and Co-operation: Striking the Right Balance, *California Management Review*, 31, 3, 25-37.

Juhel, M. H. (2000) Globalisation and Partnerships in Ports: Trends for the 21st Century, *Ports and Harbours*, 45, 5, 9-14.

Lloyd's List Maritime Asia (1999) Kwai Chung stagnates, March, 6.

Ministry of Transport (1998), *China Shipping Development Annual Report*, Beijing.

Mooney, T. (2000) Friend or foe? *Lloyd's Freight Transport Buyer Asia*, May/June, 37-38.

Port Development Board (1995) *Port Cargoes Forecasts 1995*, Hong Kong.

Port Development International (2000) Top 100 Container Ports, April, 14-15.

Rimmer, P. (1996) International Linkages and Interactions of the Emerging World Cities of Pacific Area, in Yeung, Y. M. and Fu, C. L. (eds), *Emerging World Cities in Pacific Asia*, United Nations University Press, Tokyo, 48-97.

Shippers Today (1997) Hong Kong and the Emerging Southern China Ports, July and August.

Sung, Y. W. (1991) *The China-Hong Kong Connection*, Cambridge University Press, New York.

Sung, Y. W. (1998) *Hong Kong and South China: the Economic Synergy*, City University of Hong Kong Press, Hong Kong.

Tupper, R. F. (1998) The Development of Hong Kong as a World Shipping Centre, *Proceedings of International Conference on Shipping and Shipping Market Facing 21st Century*, Shenzhen, China, 12-15 October.

Wang, J. J. (1997) Hong Kong Container Port: the South China Load Centre Under Threat, *Journal of the Eastern Asia Society for Transportation Studies*, 2, 1, 101-114.

Wong, A. K. and Beresford, A. K. (1996a) *External Threats to Hong Kong Port*, Occasional Papers No. 34, Department of Maritime Studies and International Transport, University of Wales College of Cardiff, Cardiff.

Wong, A. K. and Beresford, A. K. (1996b) *The Future of Hong Kong Port*, Occasional Papers No. 33, Department of Maritime Studies and International Transport, University of Wales College of Cardiff, Cardiff.

Wong, J. S. (1999) Hong Kong Port Boxed in by Competition, *South China Morning Post*, September 13th.

6 A Comparative Study of Sino-Korean Oil Transport by Sea

Xie Xinlian
Shipping Management College
Dalian Maritime University
Dalian, People's Republic of China
Cao Qingguang
Cosco Dalian
Dalian, People's Republic of China
Tae-Woo Lee
Division of Maritime Transportation Science
Korea Maritime University
Pusan, Korea

Introduction

Both China and South Korea need to import large amounts of crude oil at present and in the future. However, the situation in terms of oil trade and shipping operations of the two countries are quite different. The demand for sea transportation, the related shipping policy, the physical condition of the tanker fleets and the operating features of the two fleets are examined and compared in this paper. Based on these comparison and analysis, a constructive suggestion is recommended for the co-operation of the two sides in the trade and transportation area.

The Demand for Oil Transport by Sea

Korea and China are neighbouring countries located on the Pacific rim. As the distribution of world resources is uneven, South Korea has almost no proven crude oil resources and therefore needs to import a large amount of crude oil from abroad, mostly from the Middle East, each year to meet increasing domestic demand. Crude oil imports have increased in response to consumption. Import volume rose to 560.6 million barrels in 1993 from

5.8 million barrels in 1964, more than an 89 fold increase. By 1997, the amount of crude oil imported into Korea had risen to 873.4 million barrels (http://Korea.emb.washington.dc.us; Ministry of Maritime Affairs and Fisheries, 1997).

The data given in Table 6.1 and that in Tables 6.2 and 6.3 show differences in the amounts of crude oil imported to Korea. However, the size of the discrepancies are not so large as to invalidate the following analysis significantly.

Table 6.1: Crude Oil Imports to Korea

Year	1985	1990	1994	1995	1996	1997
Volume m bbl	198.3	308.4	573.7	624.5	721.9	873.4

Source: About Korea Statistics, Energy, 1997.

Table 6.2: Import Volume of Crude Oil, Korea

Year	1994	1995	1996
Revenue Ton (million ton)	57.4	80.1	94.2 (including exports)

Source: Ministry of Maritime Affairs and Fisheries, 1997.

Table 6.3: The Distribution of Crude Oil Between Ports (1996)

Port	Pusan	Inchon	Daesan	Yosu	Kwangyang	Ulsan
R/T million ton	0.4	2.8	12.7	8.4	21.1	48.9

Source: Ministry of Maritime Affairs and Fisheries, 1997.

According to a report of the EIA (United States Energy Information Administration), there are eight crude oil refineries in South Korea. The total amount of crude oil refining capacity is about 2.2 m bbl/d in 1997 (EIA, 1997), (Table 6.4). The major oil refineries of Korea consist of SK Oil Corporation (formerly Yukong Limited), Kukdong Oil Company's Refinery, LG-Caltex Oil Corporation (formerly Honam), Kyungin Energy Co. Ltd., Ssangyong Oil Refining Co. Ltd, Yochon Petrochemical Complex and Hanwha Oil, Hyundai Oil.

Table 6.4: The Capacity of Major Refineries in South Korea (1,000bbl/d)

Refinery	Ulsan	Onsan	Yocheon	Daesan	Inchon
Capacity	760	500	361	310	261

Source: EIA (1997).

SK Corporation imported and refined a total of 289 million barrels of crude oil during 1997, resulting in a daily average of 792,000 barrels. The refinery is capable of producing 876,000 barrels a day, which means it operated at 90.4 per cent of capacity over the year.

LG-Caltex Oil, Korea's first private oil refining company, inaugurated in May 1967 a joint venture with Caltex Petroleum Corporation of the United States, and its daily oil refining capacity has grown from 60,000 bbl/d in 1969 to 650,000 bbl/d today. Meanwhile, Hyundai oil was successful in its early completion of a 200,000 barrels expansion project (Phase One) in 1996.

In China however, the situation is somehow different. Crude oil production was 2.99 and 3.13 million bbl/d in 1995 and 1996 respectively (EIA, 1997). Although a large amount of crude oil is produced each year, it mainly originates in north-east China and at the same time a large amount of oil is consumed in the Central, East and South of China, along the coastline. This means that the transportation of crude oil from north to south is necessary and preferable by ships. There was also a large amount of crude oil exported mainly to Japan before 1990. Entering the 1990s, as domestic consumption increased, the crude oil produced in mainland China gradually became insufficient. The amount of exported crude oil gradually reduced whilst the amount of imported crude oil increased rapidly (Table 6.5).

Table 6.5: The Import and Export Volume of Petroleum Oil of China (10,000 ton)

	1985	1990	1991	1992	1993	1994	1995	1996	1997
Total export	3,630	3,110	2,931	2,860	2,506	2,380	2,455	2,696	2,542
Crude	3,105	2,290	2,155	2,135	1,935	1,840	1,885	2,040	1,983
Total import	90	776	1,249	2,125	3,616	2,903	3,673	4,537	5,926
Crude	-	290	595	1,130	1,560	1,230	1,709	2,262	3,547

Sources: Youfu (1998), China Statistic Year Book 1997 (1998), China Economic Year Book 1997 (1998).

China emerged as a net importer of petroleum oil in 1993 and became a net importer of crude oil in 1996. Imported crude oil comes mostly from Indonesia and the Middle East (mainly Oman, Yemen and Iran) and includes small volumes from Alaska. There are 34 crude oil refineries in China. The total amount of crude oil refining capacity is about 3.0 million bbl/d in 1997. The capacity of the seven major refineries in China is listed in Table 6.6.

Table 6.6: Capacity of Major Refineries in China (1,000bbl/d)

	Fushun	Maoming	Qilu	Gaoqiao	Dalian	Yanshan	Jinling
Capacity	174	170	160	146	142	140	134

Source: EIA (1997).

In the longer term, China is projected to be at the forefront of new Pacific Rim growth. China's current strategy is to streamline and upgrade existing refining capacity rather than build new refineries. The goal is to reach 5 million bbl/d by 2010 (EIA, 1997).

An indication of Chinese crude oil trade can be gleaned from comparing oil production (supply) and refinery throughput (demand) (Table 6.7). This comparison gives a broad indication of the likely imbalance between Chinese crude oil output and consumption.

Table 6.7: The Predicted Demand and Supply of Crude Oil in Mainland China (10,000 ton)

	2000	2010
Demand	21,000	34,000
Supply	16,500	25,000

Source: Youfu (1998).

From the above analysis we can see that both neighbouring countries need to import large amounts of crude oil each year presently and in the future and also, most of this imported crude oil currently comes and will continue to come from the Middle East. This shows the importance of oil transportation and the increasing significance of the tanker fleets of the two countries.

The Policy of Oil Transportation and its Implications

Crude oil tonnage can be just as important as the oil trade of countries with international ports either with or without sufficient domestic oil supplies. Operating oil tonnage needs special technology and a high level of management skills as well as very large capital investments. Therefore, to develop an oil fleet commonly needs government support and guidance. Government policy plays an important role in the development of the shipping industry and not least the oil tanker fleet, in any maritime country.

In terms of South Korea, the import of crude oil is very important to its economic development. In order to improve the balance of payments and at the same time, to promote the development of an ocean-going shipping industry in South Korea, the government adopted a policy of cargo reservation (the waiver system) in 1959 and this system was further developed over the coming years. In 1965, the government adopted a resolution to require that over 50 per cent of inbound cargo procured with aid, loan or other government funds should be transported aboard Korean flagged ships (Lee, 1990). The main idea of the waiver system was that imports of crude oil, coal, iron ore etc were reserved for Korean flagged vessels unless a waiver was granted to a foreign vessel by the Korean Ship-owners Association. This was very helpful in developing the South Korean tanker fleet in its early stages and from then on.

The South Korean government also emphasised the construction of infrastructure facilities very early on. According to the Heavy and Chemical Industry Development Plan set up in 1973, the South Korean government developed industrial ports to meet increasing sea-borne trade, e.g. crude oil handling and petrochemical plants. For example, the Port of Ulsan was constructed mainly to serve the oil industry and nearby petrochemical complexes.

From the beginning of crude oil imports, Korea has been heavily dependent upon Middle Eastern countries, especially Saudi Arabia and Kuwait. This gave rise to some problems during the second oil crisis and since then much effort has been made to diversify the supply of crude oil. As a result, import sources of crude oil were gradually expanded. In 1993, 30.8 per cent of the total crude oil was imported from Saudi Arabia, 13.6 per cent from Iran, 6.2 per cent from Indonesia, 4.9 per cent from Malaysia, 12.4 per cent from Oman and the remaining 32.2 per cent from Ecuador, Brunei, Mexico and other countries (http://Korea.emb.washington.dc.us).

The authorities of the country plan to reduce the oil supply from the Middle East from 78 per cent in 1997 to 65 per cent within 10 years. One example is LG-Caltex Corporation's announcement in December 1996 of a long-term contract to import 30,000 barrels per day of Alaskan North Slope oil from BP. South Korea is also building a strategic petroleum reserve in anticipation of joining the International Energy Agency (IEA). Strategic stocks are currently equivalent to a 60-day supply (the IEA requires a 90-day supply).

In January 1997, South Korea began implementing the deregulation of petroleum product prices and liberalisation of import and export markets. Government price ceilings on petroleum products were lifted (refiners were required to notify the government in advance of price increases), and non-refiners (up to 50 per cent foreign ownership) were permitted to import and export crude oil and petroleum products without the need for a government licence. Beginning January 1st 1999, any company was able to enter any level of the oil business by simply registering with the government.

With suitable policy and government guidance over many years, South Korea has established a strong tanker fleet suitable for importing crude oil for the economic development of the country.

In terms of China, as domestic oil consumption surpasses its domestic production, the import of large quantities of petroleum oil is inevitable. The Chinese authorities are likely to prefer oil imports focusing on crude rather than products trades in order to boost refinery throughput. Oil transportation by sea is mainly carried out by two shipping companies, COSCO Dalian and Haixing Co. Ltd of the China Shipping Group, which are responsible for international shipping and domestic shipping respectively. Haixing Co. Ltd developed steadily as the result of the Chinese law on cabotage, while COSCO Dalian gradually withdrew from crude oil transportation from the late 1980s to the middle of the 1990s when China switched from a planned economy to a market economy. The Chinese government wants every enterprise to enter the market on an equal footing and to stand on its own two feet. Although it is better for Chinese flagged vessels to transport imported crude oil, the government has adopted no practical measures to encourage domestic shipping companies to enter this field. As a result they have almost abandoned crude oil transportation from 1997 because of the large deficits incurred from operating tankers and the absence of any kind of subsidies from government.

As the import of crude oil continues to grow, China will also need to invest significant capital in terminals to accommodate imported crude and product cargoes. At present there is no berth for VLCCs along the coastline of mainland China, not to mention ULCCs. For this reason, single point mooring (SPM) terminals may play a growing role in the Chinese oil trade, particularly for crude imports by VLCC. Three new VLCC terminals including one quay and two SPMs are planned for Dalian, Dafeng and Qidong in Jiangsu province.

As petroleum consumption and import volumes of crude oil increase, China's government needs to recognise the importance of having a tanker fleet of suitable size in order to keep the economic development of the country stable and healthy in the long term. At present, although it is not wise in some ways to adopt a special protective policy in the maritime sector, the new system of enterprise organisation in China may give rise to a good perspective for China's tanker fleet. The new system is that all the big state enterprises including the petroleum and shipping companies, are under the guidance of the State Economic and Trade Commission.

The Development of the Tanker Fleets

Korea has three tanker fleets belong to different parent companies. The general composition of these three tanker fleets is listed in Table 6.8.

Table 6.8: South Korea Controlled Tanker Fleet (1997)

	VLCC	Suezmax	Panamax	Cape	Product	LPG	LNG
No.	17	2	1	1	8	17	3
1,000 dwt	4684	269	70	149	172	274 (cub m)	323

Source: Author.

SK Shipping (Yukong Line Limited, YKL) started transporting crude oil in 1982. Today YKL operates seven VLCCs which also includes a number of LPG/LNG/chemical carriers and the 'Yukong Navigator', which can carry 1.9 million barrels of crude oil.

Hoyu Tanker started as a wholly-owned subsidiary of the LG-Caltex Oil Corporation in 1972. Since its foundation, it has been actively involved in the transportation of imported crude oil and LPG for the LG-Caltex Oil Corporation and LG-Caltex Gas Corporation. They have five VLCC and two Suezmax vessels to transport crude oil and a number of product carriers and LPG carriers.

Hyundai Merchant Marine (HMM), founded in 1976, has over 107 vessels including full container carriers, oil tankers, car carriers, LNG carriers, bulk carriers, etc. The Gas and Crude Carrier Department was renamed Tanker Departments I and II on the 1st February 1995. Tanker Department II consists of the VLCC team and a products team that is responsible for the transport of crude oil and petroleum products world-wide, especially from the Persian Gulf to Korea. The VLCC team operates four VLCCs and is scheduled to be delivered one VLCC more by 1998. The main customers of crude carrier are Hyundai Oil Refinery Co. Ltd. and other domestic and overseas oil refineries.

As the import quantity of crude oil is very large, Korean refineries also need to charter in considerable numbers of tankers for these cargoes. For example in March 1998, SK Shipping chartered a variety of vessels listed in Table 6.9 (http://www.skshipping.com). The total size of Korea's tanker fleet between 1987 and 1996 is listed in Table 6.10 (Ministry of Maritime Affairs and Fisheries).

China's domestic transportation of crude oil began in the early 1970s with small ships, namely 15,000 dwt and 24,000 dwt vessels, which were all built in domestic shipyards. In the middle of the 1980s both the fleets for domestic and international (mainly export) transportation of crude oil developed very quickly to meet the needs of increasing economic development. The number of tankers exceeded 80 but the largest vessel had a capacity of only 75,000 dwt and was a second-hand ship. Entering the 1990s the size of the tanker fleet continued to increase for the domestic fleet but gradually reduced for the international fleet.

Table 6.9: South Korean Chartered Vessels (March 1998)

	VLCC	Aframax	Product	LPG	LNG	Handy-max	Pana-max	Cape
No.	15	4	11	2	1	35	20	15
1,000 dwt	4,300	400	447	102	72	1,225	1,300	2,250

Source: About SK Shipping (http://www.skshipping.com).

Table 6.10: Status of Korean Flagged Tankers

	1987	1988	1989	1990	1991	1992	1993	1994	1995	1996
Korea Flag (No.)	518	527	529	532	540	567	578	602	607	625
Korea Flag (GRT 1000)	1,031	1,189	733	596	692	790	699	733	582	628
BBC/HP (No.)	na	na	na	na	na	17	22	31	15	40
BBC/HP (GRT 1000)	na	na	na	na	na	543	1,075	1,074	1,593	1,667

Note: na – not available; BBC/HP – Bareboat Charter.
Source: Author.

In 1995, the Chinese controlled tanker fleet numbered 51 vessels of five million dwt, as detailed in Table 6.11. Some 82 per cent of tankers are less than 100,000 dwt in size. By far the most popular vessel within the Chinese-controlled tanker fleet is the Panamax unit between 50-75,000 dwt.

Hong Kong also had 51 tankers of 10 m dwt at the end of march 1995, as shown in Table 6.12. In 1995, the Ocean Tramping Co. Ltd had one vessel of 281,751 dwt and Hong Kong Ming Wah Shipping had seven vessels of 2,057,875 dwt (total: eight vessels of 2,339,626 dwt). Hong Kong Ming Wah operated the bulk of Chinese owned VLCCs and China's only ULCC. The turbine tanker 'New Explorer', 390,038 dwt, was delivered from the NKK yard in 1976.

Table 6.11: The Chinese Controlled Tanker Fleet by Size

	Number of vessels	dwt
10-50,000 dwt	6	164,588
50-110,000 dwt	36	2,503,983
110-200,000 dwt	1	146,041
200,000+	8	2,399,626
Total	51	5,154,238

Source: Drewry Shipping Consultants.

China has 116 tankers amounting to 5.39 million dwt and their average age is 16.6 years, whilst the average age of the world tanker fleet was about 14.9 years at 1st January 1997 (Cottew, 1997).

In comparison with the growth of imported petroleum oil demand, China's present crude carrying capacity, especially the larger size vessels, will be insufficient to handle the projected growth in Chinese oil imports. As a result, chartered-in tonnage will play a major role in satisfying both China's crude and product requirements.

Table 6.12: Hong Kong Tanker Fleet by Size

1,000 dwt	Number	Dwt	%
45-90	16	1,227	12.2
90-125	5	483	4.8
125-175	1	146	1.5
175-300	26	7,166	71.6
300+	3	994	9.9
Total	51	10,017	100

Source: Drewry Shipping Consultants.

Operating Comparisons of the Two Country's Tanker Fleets

The tanker fleets of South Korea are mainly used for carrying imports and exports of oil to and from that country. The primary reason why the Korean tanker fleets are able to obtain Korean oil cargoes is the waiver system which was mentioned earlier in this paper. Another reason is that they belong to different, large company groups, which also own and operate oil refineries. In this way, the Korean ship-owners can secure cargo from domestic shippers. The shipping company often signs a long-term contract for oil transportation with a refinery including for example, HMM's Tanker Dept. II which has a long-term contract with a domestic oil company. It is notable that this type of co-operation between ship-owner and shipper is very good for the country's economy, namely its foreign currency balance.

Whilst the Korean oil companies mainly employ a crude oil fleet as part of their own group by engaging in long-term contracts, China's oil refinery companies frequently charter VLCCs in recent years from Hong Kong or other ship-owners to transport their oil cargo acquired on the spot market.

Taking 1994 for example, Sinochem chartered 35 vessels to haul 30 dirty and five clean product cargoes of 4.81m dwt. Of the dirty cargoes carried, 47 per cent were shipped in VLCC tonnage, 10 per cent in Suezmax, 27 per cent in Aframax, 10 per cent in Panamax and 7 per cent in smaller tankers. All refined product cargoes were transported in tankers of less than 35,000 dwt. Unipec chartered 24 vessels to haul dirty and clean cargoes of 3.05m dwt; 61 per cent of the 23 dirty cargoes were loaded in the Arabian Gulf. Nine VLCC and one Suezmax units were used on these voyages. China Oil chartered 24 tankers to move cargoes of 1.505m dwt. Some 13 voyages were made using Aframax tonnage. In summary, the crude oil fleet under Chinese control is very rarely used to meet China's oil import requirements. Chinese state refineries tend to charter foreign VLCCs to import crude.

These facts have again reflected the role of a protectionist policy in the maritime field from a different angle. On the one hand, the domestic, coastal transportation of oil in China is protected by the cabotage law. As a result the fleet has developed steadily from the early 1970s to today. On the other hand, the development policy of the Chinese fleet for international oil transportation is quite different. In the 1980s, the tankers employed on international routes leading to China were mainly for the export of crude oil from China. Although they developed very quickly throughout the 1980s, their competitive ability is comparatively weak. Therefore, when the amount of export crude reduced, the tanker fleet was also reduced considerably. As an independent ship-owner with no special beneficial relationship to any refinery, COSCO does not directly own any VLCC/ULCC tonnage preferring to run a fleet out of Hong Kong, Meanwhile, China's VLCCs are chiefly on time charter to international oil companies including Ssangyong – the South Korean refiner.

As mentioned previously, oil consumption is likely to increase substantially over the next decade. The Middle East offers the most viable solution to China's future oil demand growth. Chinese reported dirty, spot trading activity accounted for a 4 per cent share or 2.55m dwt of the Arabian Gulf/Red Sea-Far East trade in 1994. To put this into perspective, such a level equates to approximately 51,210 bbl/d – some 15-20 per cent of Chinese crude oil imports during 1994. VLCCs, and to a lesser extent ULCCs, may prove to be the most cost effective form of transporting crude oil from the Arabian Gulf to China.

The problems faced by the Chinese ship-owners may hopefully be settled from now on because the state shipping companies and the state refineries are under the jurisdiction of the same economic and trade commission. The new relationship between enterprises in different industries in China is helpful in improving the current situation. It is possible to reconcile the existing contradictions between shipper and ship-owner in oil transportation under these new relationships, at least in theory.

Conclusions

The two neighbouring countries of Korea and China need to import large amounts of crude oil at present and for the foreseeable future and in that sense face a similar scenario. However, the situation in terms of the tanker fleet controlled by the two countries is quite different. While Korea can supply tanker vessels to third parties around the world, mainland China is in contrast, short of large tankers (VLCC).

Being the largest international shipping company in China, Cosco needs to make a decision at this moment about either directly or through its Hong Kong based subsidiaries, to invest in and operate a crude oil tanker fleet, preferably VLCCs and ULCCs, serving the increasing imports of crude oil of mainland China. Because of their lack of experience in running this type of vessel, it is perhaps more realistic to time or bareboat charter some VLCCs before going on to build its own vessels later. In November 1998, we witness the first VLCC of 250,000 dwt to come into operation for China. This vessel is chartered in by a newly formed oil transporting company which is jointly owned by the China Shipping Group and CMB of Belgium. There is no doubt that this is the beginning for Chinese mainland ship-owners in developing a VLCC fleet.

South Korean interests have steadily become involved in running a tanker fleet, including VLCCs and various other types of vessels for many years. They have not only a strong tanker fleet serving the country but also the experience of running it. The influence of the Asian crisis resulted in a reduction of consumption of oil in Korea and therefore the country has sufficient crude fleet to find new business on the world market. This introduces the possibility of co-operation and possibly the exchange of oil tonnage between the shipping companies of the two countries.

As one of the results of this research, we would also like to give a constructive suggestion about the co-operation of the tanker fleets of the two countries. Our suggestion is to form an alliance in oil trade and transportation to keep the supply of sea-borne oil stable and at the same time to reduce the costs of oil transportation to a minimum. This will be beneficial to both sides in the long run.

References

About SK Shipping, http://www.skshipping.com.

China Economic Year Book 1997 (1998) China Economic Year Book Publishing House.

China Statistic Year Book 1997 (1998) China Statistic Publishing House.

Cottew, T. (1997) *The Present Status and Future Prospects of Tanker Shipping Market – the Intertanko View,* 6th Asia Pacific Sea transport Conference, Hong Kong.

Drewry Shipping Consultants (1995) *China and World shipping*, Research Report.

E.I.A. (1997) *Reports of China and South Korea*, Energy Information Administration, November 1997.

http://Korea.emb.washington.dc.us/.

Lee, T-W. (1990) Korean Shipping Policy: the Role of Government, *Marine Policy,* September.

Ministry of Maritime Affairs and Fisheries (1997) *Statistical Year Book of Maritime Affairs and Fisheries.*

Youfu, S. (1998) *The Good Perspective of China Oil Transportation Market*, Shipping Review, January 1st.

7 COSCO Restructuring

Mingnan Shen
Shipping Management College
Dalian Maritime University
Dalian, People's Republic of China
Tae-Woo Lee
Division of Maritime Transportation Science
Korea Maritime University
Pusan, Korea

Introduction

Since 1978, when China adopted the radical economic policy of 'opening up to the outside world while reforming inside', significant political and economic changes have taken place which have had great impact on the development of Chinese shipping and for example, the China Ocean Shipping (Group) Company (COSCO). This study aims to examine the process of restructuring of COSCO during the period of Chinese economic transition, from the planning to the market economic system.

Since the open door policy adopted by the Chinese government in 1978, China has undergone a radical transformation of her economy from planning to the market system. Significant political and economic changes have taken place. China has grown to be one of the leading ship-owning countries in the world with the deregulation of its shipping policy (which included the opening of the market to foreign shipping companies as well as the loosening of controls on domestic shipping companies), the ensuing growth process having had significant impact on the development of Chinese shipping and particularly COSCO. In order to cope with the changing political, economic and world shipping environment, COSCO has continued to restructure its organisation system and strategy.

The purpose of this study is to examine the process of restructuring COSCO in the period of Chinese economic transition from a planned to a market system, focusing on the period 1979-1999. This study used a literature survey to examine the development of Chinese economic reform and Chinese shipping. A number of questionnaires were distributed among the financial, personnel, planning, researching and fleet management departments of COSCO and its branches. The questions were based on why and how they reorganised structures at each phase of the economic transition period. Interviews with the managers in COSCO and officials in the Ministry of Communication (MOC) were also conducted to obtain their opinions and data on restructuring.

Reviews of Chinese Economic Reform and the Changes to Shipping in China

Phases of Chinese Economic Reform

1949-78: The planning system Following the transformation to socialist ownership in the early 1950s, the centralised planning system was established by co-operation between the Chinese State Planning Commission and Soviet experts, based along Stalinist Soviet line in China. In 1953, China launched its first Five Year Plan (1953-57) based on the Soviet model. This system had the following characteristics. Firstly, the most important industrial enterprises were owned by the state. Secondly, enterprises' economic activities were controlled within a highly centralised model of mandatory planning. Thirdly, resource allocation and product provision were co-ordinated by the state planner. Finally, the employment and wage system were formulated by the state.

From 1958, moral encouragement was given primacy over material incentives and 'politics in command' became the main theme of Chinese management. Output per unit of capital invested declined 25 per cent between 1952 and 1978 and over-centralised management, irrational investment decisions by bureaucrats and poor labour motivation were identified as being the primary reasons for the industry's failure.[1]

The crucial failures of the central planning system in China could be identified thus. A shortage of commodities occurred because enterprises arranged their production according to the state plan, having little incentive to produce non-plan commodities. The planning and control processes became political and bureaucratic as enterprises were administered by both central and local government. Managers, helpless because economic activities were controlled by the state, felt no need to improve performance. The lack of incentives and the penalties for enterprise managers and workers promoted resources wastage with consequential, poor performance. Finally, the organisational structure in China was overly complex with performance assessment involving the central planning system, the party organisation and the production-technical system.[2]

1979-83: The stagnant phase On December 22, 1978, at the third plenary session of the 11th National Congress of the Chinese Communist Party, the Party officially announced its plan for economic reform. In April 1979 it was decided to implement a plan of 'readjustment, reform, remedy and improvement'. The reform began in the rural areas, based on the Household Responsibility System.[3] After the 'freeing up' of the rural markets in 1979, all components of farm output grew more rapidly, especially cash crops and animal husbandry.[4] A number of township and village enterprises were founded on the basis of the then-surplus labour and capital.[5]

From 1979 the state-owned enterprise (SOE) reform was initiated and some pilot programmes were implemented in selected regions such as Sichuan. Key elements were the decentralisation of administrative powers to the provinces and municipalities, the development of market relations, the delegation of responsibility for performance to enterprise managers and the encouragement of incentive systems. A system allowing some retention of profit was introduced to create a link between enterprise performance and reward. There were new forms of investment financing and opportunities for enterprises to use depreciation funds were improved. In 1983, the government began to substitute tax payments for profit retention, with the enterprises paying a progressive profit tax up to 55 per cent.[6]

In 1979, four Special Economic Zones were established, and the 'Law of the PRC on Chinese Foreign Joint Ventures' was promulgated. The basic motivation of this was to promote inflows of foreign investment and technology, as well as managerial techniques. According to the Ministry of Foreign Trade and Economic Co-operation's statistics from 1979 to 1983, 638 joint ventures had been established at the initial stage of the open door policy.

1984-88: Accelerated development phase Between 1984 and 1988 there were dramatic changes in China's reform policies. SOEs became the focus of the reform and decentralisation was formally adopted as the programme on a national scale. The concept of market was accepted in official ideology. In 1984 the State Council issued the 'Provisional Regulations on the Enlargement of Autonomy of State Industrial Enterprises'. These regulations expanded the decision-making powers of SOEs in ten areas, e.g. production planning, product marketing, pricing of products outside the state plan and materials purchasing. In that same year, according to the 'Decision on Reform of Economic Structure',[7] certain enterprises were released from central Ministry control and some prices were permitted to float. SOEs became independent and responsible for their own profit and loss and capable of transforming and developing themselves. In 1986 the Economic Contract Responsible System (ECRS) was introduced to medium-sized and large SOEs. Under ECRS, an enterprise's income tax liability and profit remittances was determined by the provisions of the enterprise's contract with the government.

In order to attract more foreign investment, 14 coastal cities were opened in 1984 and the average annual growth rate of joint ventures at this phase achieved 52 per cent.

1989-91: Adjustment phase As the economic institutions were transferred from central planning to a mixed economy, the environment became turbulent and unstable. Post 1985 the economy became overheated with an annual inflation rate of over 17 per cent which started to threaten the price reforms after the government introduced a dual-price system.[8] Since September 1988, the government decided to resume central control over enterprise management and the economic environment. It reduced investment, partly through administrative directives and partly by cutting the money supply and re-extended the range of direct price controls and subsidies. Inflation was sharply reduced and a current account deficit was turned into a surplus by 1990.

1992-present: Introduction of the market system From 1987 to 1992, the ECRS was the principal scheme in the reform of SOEs. However, the effectiveness of the system as a measure to improve SOEs performance was unreliable.[9] The reforms after 1992 were aimed at clarifying the ownership structure and introducing new enterprise governance based on the market economy. The reform focused on the experience of modern enterprise institutions, meaning the shareholder committee, the board of directors and the supervisory board.

Under the '1988 Enterprise Law' and its implementation regulations,[10] and the '1993 Company Law' implemented in July 1994, SOEs may restructure themselves into shareholding enterprises. Issuance of shares or corporatisation transforms them into legal entities that are distinct from the state bureaucracy. It separates state ownership rights from administrative and regulatory powers and ministerial oversight from enterprise management.[11]

Along with corporatisation, 55 enterprises were authorised by the Chinese government to establish enterprise groups in 1989 including

COSCO. Each group consisted of a core enterprise that was linked to other enterprises through shareholdings into a large conglomerate. It may invest in new and existing enterprises. Its shareholdings and scope of operations may extend beyond the administrative boundary of a single ministry or government unit for greater economies of scale and scope.

Changes within Shipping in China

The Growth of Chinese Ocean Shipping (COSCO) under the Planning System

When the People's Republic of China was founded in October 1949, its shipping industry was in a state of total disarray. China was politically and economically isolated in the 1950s and early 1960s. It had few diplomatic and trade relations with non-communist countries. China did, however, receive substantial economic and technical assistance from the former USSR and other traditional socialist countries to develop its shipping industry and, not surprisingly, followed the Soviet model of planning – characterised by highly centralised and rigid government controls with mandatory production targets. Shipping was treated as an important element of national policy and the aims of developing the Chinese ocean shipping industry were as follows, [12]

- To satisfy the needs of its own foreign trade;
- To satisfy the development of diplomatic relationship with other countries;
- To build up the international position of the country; and
- To reduce reliance upon foreign flag fleets.

Chinese shipping services did not resume until the Overseas Transport Company, China National Chartering Corporation[13] and the Chinese-Polish Joint Stock Shipping Company were formed in early 1950s. Overseas Chinese were allowed to operate as private agents for seagoing vessels in order to encourage them to participate in China's shipping to facilitate development. An agreement was signed with Czechoslovakia in 1955 with full powers granted to them to operate and purchase vessels for the Chinese government.

With rapid and sustained economic growth, the Chinese seaborne trade increased approximately fivefold between 1952 and 1958, from 2.24

million tons to 11.58 million tons. However, despite the growth of Chinese shipping tonnage, Chinese seaborne trade was still heavily dependent upon foreign carriers. According to the statistics for 1958 and 1959, the annual chartering tonnage was over 1 million US$. Chinese operators carried less than 20 per cent of the total volume in 1958.

To cut down the expenditure of foreign currency on chartering foreign vessels and to promote the expansion of the national fleet, raising the share of the Chinese flag in foreign trades, it was considered necessary to establish a national shipping company for the Chinese government. COSCO was conceived and on April 27, 1961 its Guangzhou branch was established, operating a fleet of 25 vessels of about 229,200 dwt.

In 1964, the Chinese government decided to purchase second-hand vessels with overseas floating capital of the Bank of China, to develop the ocean shipping fleet, it being perceived to be more reasonable to purchase vessels rather than rely on chartered vessels from abroad. A favourable policy designed to support the national fleet ranging from tax exemptions and financial support, to cargo preference and planned shipbuilding, was set up. The policy included:

- Deferred loan and interests repayment (within the first 5 years after the loans had been collected there was no need to commence the repayment of the loan or interests).
- Exclusion from the national physical taxation planning of all revenue accrued from the vessel brought or built with the loan collected (it was after the completion of the repayment of the loan that revenue from such vessels was included in the national physical taxation planning).
- To guarantee the repayment of the loan on time (the vessels were granted priority in the allocation of cargoes for export and import).
- These vessels had priority of loading and unloading when in the ports of China.

In 1978, the total tonnage of the Chinese ocean-going fleet reached approximately 6 million GT. China had ended the era of relying wholly on leasing foreign vessels for her ocean transport.

The Introduction of Competition in Chinese Shipping

The reforms in China's shipping sector have been introduced in the context of the overall economic reform programme initiated since the late 1970s. For the past two decades China has continuously expanded, opening new fields of commerce, introducing foreign funding, technology and advanced management and brought about competitive mechanisms which have played an active role in establishing China's shipping market mechanism and the development of China's shipping business.

Since 1978, the Chinese government has been continuously expanding ports and opening them to the outside world. The number of China's open ports has increased from 16 in 1978 to more than 130 by 2000. In 1984, foreign shipping companies were allowed to operate international container liner services linked with these ports and 70 foreign shipping companies had opened up such lines in Chinese ports by the end of 2000. From over 2,900 short sea voyages and 300 major ocean going voyages in and out of China, foreign shipping companies occupy respectively 44 per cent and 71 per cent of the market share.

A series of active port opening policies also have been set to promote Chinese port construction/development since 1992, such as encouraging China-overseas joint construction and operation of loading/unloading businesses at public terminals. Sea-Land Service, P&O, Hutchison and others have been involved in China's port development and operations projects.[14]

In 1984, all Chinese shipping companies were allowed to engage in ocean shipping business and competitive mechanisms were introduced to promote ocean shipping service standards. In 1986 foreign shipping companies were also allowed to establish representative offices in China to advertise their services and contract business for their parent companies. Over 450 representative offices had been established by 2000.[15]

In 1987, foreign investors were allowed to establish shipping companies in China by way of joint venture or co-operation based on the principle in favour of introducing fund, technology and advanced management. These companies could operate vessels flying the Chinese flag and conduct international, coastal and inland water transport. Since 1992, in accordance with governmental bilateral marine transport or consultation among marine authorities, foreign shipping companies have been allowed to establish shipping companies exclusively owned by themselves in China to provide such businesses as canvassing cargo, issuing B/L, settling freight and signing transport service contracts. At present, China has authorised 21 foreign companies to establish exclusively foreign owned shipping companies and more than 50 branch ones. Further to these opening policies, in 1997, China launched pilot projects through exclusively foreign owned, container transport service companies allowing them to conduct seven kinds of businesses (those engaged in booking, stuffing and un-stuffing of containers, storing, issuing of goods receipts, collection of freight and other authorised charges, maintaining containers and equipment and connecting and signing transport service contracts with truck companies).[16]

Since 1988, by revoking all kinds of subsidies to domestic carries through administrative means, the freight forwarding market has also been gradually opened. Foreign lines have been able to canvass cargo in China since the end of 1991 with the result that their businesses are flourishing. This in turn has provided an incentive to Chinese shipping companies who have themselves embarked upon major upgrading which, in turn, has increased the competition.[17] Policy on shipping finance has also kept abreast of change and is regularly adjusted with the development of Chinese economic reform. Before 1992, shipping and shipbuilding enterprises directly under the control of the MOC paid an annual interest rate of 3.6 per cent for any loan from a domestic bank, a rate that was much lower than other shipping companies. In 1992, the Chinese government revoked this shipbuilding subsidy and discount loans were granted to shipping companies: the interest rate on the loan having been adjusted to as low as 12.3 per cent by the end of 1996. Chinese shipping companies were permitted to build ships abroad with foreign shipping finance. It could be claimed that up to 80 per cent of Chinese merchant ships were built abroad with foreign loans between 1994 and 1996. Since the Chinese shipping market steadily opened to the world, all shipping companies have to manage their activities and plan development in the same way as other business enterprises.

The Establishment of Shanghai Shipping Exchange

Despite rapid developments, due to the lack of an effective administration in China, severe damage to the interests of both ship operators and cargo owners by underground freight forwarding companies emerged in the early 1990s.[18] In 1996 the Shanghai Shipping Exchange was established jointly by the MOC and Shanghai Municipal Government to address the unhealthy maritime freight market. The main objectives of the Exchange were to regulate shipping market behaviour, adjust shipping prices and convey market information. Still a non-profit institutional legal entity, it has adopted the presidential responsibility system under the leadership of a board of directors, the members of which are drawn from ship operators, cargo owners, freight forwarders and port operators. On a trial basis, so far the Exchange is a regional market whose members consist of only those operating in Shanghai and its two neighbouring coastal provinces of Zhejiang and Jinagsu. Under the regulations of the MOC, all the shipping companies that file their tariffs with Shanghai Shipping Exchange have to fulfil specific procedures. Shanghai Shipping Exchange, in the light of the actual situation of the market and reasonable demands from the shipping companies, selected the European and Japanese routes to co-ordinate and stabilise freight rates. The Exchange has played an important role in establishing a healthy maritime freight market on the east coast of China.[19]

Formation of the Shipping Group

By 1990, China's maritime business had grown to include about 250 ocean-going shipping companies and many coastal and inland transport companies. China's ocean going fleet had reached about 20 million DWT.[20] As corporatisation had proceeded in other industries in China since the late 1980s, the MOC issued a series of documents of direction, such as 'Main Points on Deepening Enterprise Reform and Transforming its Management Mechanism' in 1993 to improve the process. Corporatisation has given the shipping companies greater independence in economic and managerial matters.

The COSCO Group and China Changjiang Shipping Corporation were established in January and March of 1993 respectively. Encouraged by the success of these two companies, the China Shipping Group (China Shipping) was founded in July 1997. These three largest state-owned shipping conglomerates, taking shipping as their core business, have engaged in various fields such as seafarer services, ship agency, freight forwarding, industry, telecommunication, supplying and trading of fuel and materials, international trade, investment and logistics service, tourism, real estate and so on.

Restructuring of COSCO

Organisation of COSCO under the Planned Economic System

Under the planned economic system, Chinese SOEs were grouped according to industry under various ministries with each industrial ministry operating its own company. Since its establishment in 1961, COSCO had been under the control of the Ocean Shipping Bureau of the MOC, which was also referred to as COSCO headquarters. Therefore COSCO had a dual role firstly as a government department responsible for developing and implementing Chinese ocean shipping policy once it was adopted by the government and secondly, as the unique state-owned ocean shipping company responsible for offering transport services for all of China.

As a government department directed by the MOC, COSCO was in charge, for example, of the management and development of national ocean shipping, improvement of co-operation with foreign countries, co-ordinating ship acquisitions, formulating marine contracts between governments and negotiating international shipping transport agreements. As an enterprise, COSCO was in charge of the management of its branches, including matters such as the distribution of cargoes and operating routes to each branch.

With the rapid development of foreign trade, COSCO had continuously expanded its fleet and organisation. On April 1st 1964, the second branch of COSCO (Shanghai) opened for business, starting with five vessels allocated by the Shanghai Maritime Bureau. In the 1970s three more branches were established which were COSCO Tianjin, COSCO Qingdao and COSCO Dalian. The organisational structure of COSCO and its branches were formed under the direction of the MOC, consisting of the departments of planning, commercial, operating, technical, general affairs, and crew.

As a consequence of the responsibilities shouldered by COSCO, and as a government department, it had practically no effective control over its investment and pricing policies. Meanwhile, being an enterprise, COSCO had been given little commercial freedom, carrying on the various obligations imposed on it by central government in pursuit of its social objectives.

Separation from the Ministry

In order to meet the needs of developing foreign economic relations and trade, a set of reform measures had been drawn up which concerned the administration of the international ocean shipping industry in China since the late 1970s. The political decision to withdraw both financially and administratively from many sectors in shipping led to increased competition between shipping companies and a wide divergence in performance standards and services has emerged. Shipping companies have to meet and react to market demands to survive in such a competitive environment.

In 1982, MOC closed the Ocean Shipping Bureau to simplify the administrative structure. In 1984 it issued a 'Notice on Reforming the Administrative System of International Shipping', announcing that COSCO was independent from MOC and able to concentrate on commercial activities. Since that time COSCO has been given the right to design its structure and strategy to cope with the fierce competition in the gradually emerging shipping market in China. The MOC has become primarily an administrative and regulatory government department responsible for formulating the policies, guidelines, regulations and statistical surveys regarding the administration of shipping companies and shipping agencies, and would no longer be empowered to engage directly in COSCO's operations.

Restructuring Fleet Management

Prior to 1984 services provided by COSCO had been split between COSCO Shanghai, Guangzhou, Dalian, Tianjin and Qingdao and this resulted in unnecessary duplication of certain management functions (at higher cost). The structure of COSCO's operating lines and liner tonnage was also multi-departmental and thus unnecessary competition was generated between the branches of COSCO. Meanwhile the maintenance of some non-profitable lines also gave rise to unnecessary cost increases.

Hence, according to the characteristics of the fleet types and routes operated by each branch, COSCO restructured its fleet management in November 1984. COSCO Tianjin, Shanghai and Guangzhou were organised as a comprehensive company mainly operating container and general cargo ships. COSCO Dalian and Qingdao specialised in management of tanker and bulk carriers respectively. The operating routes of each comprehensive company distributed by COSCO were as follows:

- COSCO Tianjin: China-East and West Africa, the Mediterranean and the Black Sea; and Tianjin and Hebei-Japan and Southeast Asia;
- COSCO Shanghai: China-USA, Australia and New Zealand; Shanghai and Tianjin-West Europe; China's east coast ports-Japan and Southeast Asia; and China's north coast ports-Hong Kong container liner trade; and
- COSCO Guangzhou: China-Iran, the Red Sea; China's ports (Shanghai and Tianjin)-West Europe; and China's south coast ports-Japan, Southeast Asia, and Hong Kong container liner trade.

COSCO manages the distribution of imports to each branch and the formulation of freight. Branches were given the right to operate exports and transportation including canvassing cargo and arranging shipment. Through restructuring fleet management, the quantity of goods transported increased by 19.38 per cent from 49.38 million tons in 1984 to 58.95 million tons in 1985.

Formation of Forwarding Companies

As the shipping market gradually opened from 1984, shipping companies have mushroomed in China. The national cargo reservation system was abandoned according to the free market economy principle in 1988. As a result the competition among shipping firms in China became much more intense because in addition, foreign competitors gained access to the Chinese market. Furthermore, trading agencies were permitted by the government to compete with each other. So, COSCO not only had to compete for business with an increasing number of shipping companies in China, but also had to negotiate with the forwarding agents and trading companies directly. The result was that COSCO's main shipping business quickly lost ground to domestic and foreign competitors and its market share of Chinese foreign trade fell from over a half to about 20 per cent.

With the need to survive and cope with this fierce competition COSCO started its forwarding business in 1985 with its four branches canvassing cargo for their fleet and responding more effectively to its customers' demands. In 1988 the individual forwarding business departments of each branch separated and were established as independent forwarding companies.

In 1988 the monthly cargo distribution meeting of the Ministry of Foreign Trade and Economic Co-operation and the MOC[21] was cancelled following the principle of reduction of government administration for enterprises. COSCO's cargoes were no longer guaranteed by the state. Thus, the process of expanding the forwarding business was greatly accelerated and by 1992 COSCO had set up 16 forwarding companies with 111 forwarding offices; its door-to-door service was made available in almost every major city, port and county throughout China. These companies specialised in fields which included space booking, customs declarations, applications for inspections, stuffing and un-stuffing, warehousing, consolidation and distribution services, ship chartering, heavy-lift cargo transportation, sea-land and sea-rail transportation and barge services. Since 1990 COSCO has engaged in airfreight forwarding and to expand its overseas business it has also established forwarding centres in Western Europe, North America and Southeast Asia. Cargo canvassed by the forwarding companies of COSCO had increased 35 per cent annually by 1992.

Establishment of the Group

Approved by the State Planning Commission, State Economic and Trade Commission and the State Structural Reform Commission on February 16th 1993, COSCO was firmly established as a shipping group, its objectives being to 'change the operational mechanism of the company and to establish a modern company system'. It had embarked on a process of 'corporatisation' in the way the group was organised, while extending its business activities beyond shipping, into land based businesses and air transport. Its headquarters was appointed as a holding company, and PENAVICO, China Marine Bunker Supply Company, COSCO Guangzhou, Shanghai, Dalian, Tianjin, Shenzhen, and Xiamen[22] as its main subsidiary companies. These subsidiary companies constituted individual economic units, connected and controlled by means of capital to the core enterprise, which owns the main share of their assets. As operating companies, they have their own management as well as choice of field and subject of operation and should cover commitments arising as a consequence of their activities.

The appointment of COSCO headquarters as the holding company is primarily:

- To improve economic effectiveness;
- To ensure administration and management of finances;
- To keep pace with increasing competition, by more flexible and active market operations;
- To improve operational decision-making; and
- To increase the chances of attracting foreign capital interested in participating in particular enterprises.

Although COSCO had continued to restructure its fleet management organisation and expanded its forwarding business since the shipping market gradually opened in China, its corporate structure was designed for the planned instead of the market economy. This management style left the centralised COSCO Group muscle-bound and unable to compete effectively with the more nimble-footed foreign operators entering China or the more efficient of China's home grown carriers, particularly those far-sighted enough to have attracted joint venture skills and capital, principally via Hong Kong. Therefore in 1995, COSCO decided to spin off operations into specialist functions operated by each of the main subsidiaries with a view to increasing productivity, cutting costs, improving services and to achieve economies of scale.[23] It divided its domestic subsidiary companies into 11 business lines comprising container transport, bulk transport, logistics, human resources, finance and insurance, manufacturing, real estate, tourism, air trade and information technology.

Restructuring Domestic Business

Before 1992 the fleet of COSCO had been managed by the branches based in the main domestic ports from Guangzhou to Dalian. These suited the old-fashioned planning economy but proved to be inefficient in a market economy. In order to increase the flexibility of organisational structures and create larger scales of operation COSCO underwent the process of restructuring its fleet management which had existed since the group was established.

The reform of COSCO's container shipping and bulk shipping lines was undertaken following the same principle. A new enterprise was established in Beijing to handle marketing and operations whilst ship management remained with the port companies. Then, after a period of 'centralised operation and decentralised management', a deeper restructuring was undertaken involving the transfer of all assets used in these operations to the new companies.

In 1993, COSCO Container Lines was established in Beijing (in a move to apply the advantages of centralised operation of containerships and scale operation) and took over the container ships operated by COSCO Guangzhou, Tianjin and Shanghai. The establishment of COSCO Container Lines helped to bring about unified management, rationalised arrangement for carrying capacity, shortened lines, faster ship turnover and enhanced competitiveness. The return of scale operation was achieved, i.e. the frequency of container service has increased to 300 sailings per month from the former 183 sailings monthly and the carrying capacity has risen to 3 million TEUs in 1995 from the previous annual 1.88 million. By 1995, eight 3,800 TEU and five 3,500 TEU fourth generation ships had been put into operation.

The strategic alliances set up by foreign carriers including APL, Maersk and others are strong competition for COSCO Container Lines. In order to carry out integration of operation and management to meet the challenges of globalisation, COSCO Container Lines merged with COSCO Shanghai in 1997, bringing an end to a four-year experiment of running all its operations of bulk, general cargo and container transportation from COSCO headquarters.[24] COSCO Container Lines adopted the principle of restructuring to a functional basis and established five divisions that included those of China, North America, Europe, the Far East and Oceania. Recently, in adherence to the market-oriented and customer-centred marketing concept, COSCO has transformed its headquarters into a centre of instruction, decision-making, information, human resources exchange, cost control and profit calculation and established a marketing sales and operation system comprising the four regional centres in China, North America, Europe and Asia-Pacific.

In a similar way, COSCO Bulk Limited, with jointly investors of eight ocean shipping companies affiliated to the COSCO Group, was set up at the end of 1995 and merged with COSCO Tianjin in 1997. Since that year, general cargo ships have been managed by COSCO Guangzhou, with tankers by COSCO Dalian.

In 1995 COSCO completed the restructuring of its freight forwarding operation and established COSCO International Freight Forwarding which was designed to tighten control over service and brand image with the entire centralised structure reporting to the headquarters of COSCO

Container Lines.[25] By 1997 COSCO International Freight Forwarding had set up 303 offices throughout China, under seven branches: Guangzhou, Dalian, Shanghai, Qingdao, Tianjin, Wuhan and Xian.

Whilst restructuring its assets to create larger-scale operations, since 1993 COSCO has expanded its land-based industries into new fields such as real estate, trade, tourism, finance and labour exchange.

In 1994 it established the COSCO Industry Corporation engaged in ship repair, facility processing, ship scrapping, container manufacture and electricity plant, as well as consolidated its terminal operation, air freight forwarding and manning businesses. In 1993, the revenues generated from its land-based industry made up 24 per cent of the total revenue of the group and the revenues increased by more than 35 per cent annually from 1994 to 1999. The land-based industry has become a pillar of the COSCO Group.

Reform of the Management System of Overseas Companies

Since COSCO opened its first representative office at Port Said in June of 1963, its overseas companies had grown to 115 by 1992. In 1993 COSCO began to adjust and rationalise the organisational and managerial system of overseas subsidiaries to expand its share of the international market. It changed the budget system with which these subsidiaries had operated under the planned economy into an independent profit centre system. By 1997, with Beijing as its home base for the overseas network, the overseas coverage of COSCO had grown to 179 offices consisting of the wholly-owned companies, joint centres and shipping representative offices under eight regional centres in Europe, North America, Australia, Africa, West Asia, Japan, Singapore and Hong Kong. In addition to becoming involved in the core business of sea traffic and maritime related business, they are expanding their business into financial affairs, trade, insurance, real estate, tourism and information technology.

In the case of Hong Kong, there were 20 wholly-owned and 29 joint ventures under COSCO before 1992, specialised in ship repair, trade, terminal operation, warehousing, and freight forwarding. In 1994, COSCO (Hong Kong) was established, merging with the existing collection of small companies. Since then, it has rationalised its operation of wholly-owned companies, joint ventures, partnerships and co-operative enterprises into five industries that are shipping, listed companies, industry, trade and forwarding in business operations. Besides the five backbone industries it has established agency businesses for vessels, cargo forwarding, trade, supply, industry, energy, finance and insurance, information and technology, manning, tourism, hotels and some others.[26]

Some Problems in the Process of Restructuring

However, at a time when reform over large state-owned shipping enterprises has made substantial progress, the years of state planning and administrative interference from government have clearly placed a heavy burden on SOEs, producing a lack of vigour in the ocean shipping industry in the country. Overstaffing, a problem that the company has far from overcome, has been regarded as a real problem in the reformation of SOEs in China.[27] COSCO has 80,000 employees on its books, but 20,000 are actually hired out to other shipping lines and it is not permitted to fire them because of the government's concerns about social stability.

Another problem COSCO faces is the cost and burden of taking care of its employees' social needs. Since 1994, the government has encouraged SOEs to adopt a 'modern enterprise system', allowing the companies to free themselves of the responsibilities of building schools, hospitals and retirement homes that they had otherwise to provide. However, the government lacks the political will to push the plan through, leaving COSCO and hundreds of other large SOEs burdened.

Conclusion

Through functional separation between government and its enterprises, marketisation, economic regulations and corporatisation, Chinese economic reform has had substantial impact upon the development of its shipping industry in many ways. It has permitted the expansion and opening of shipping markets. It has been responsible for increased competition and the restructuring of shipping enterprises. COSCO itself has re-emerged from an inefficient government subsidiary to an independent commercial entity based on Chinese Corporate Law with this rapid process exhibiting peculiarities such as gradualism, experimentation and decentralisation, all of which reflect the Chinese approach to economic reforms.

Looking to the new millennium, COSCO has to continue to take new opportunities and face new challenges ahead of it. China's entry into the WTO in 2001 is expected to increase service opportunities whilst at the same time sharpening competition. Another chance is China's 'develop-the-west' strategy, which has provided opportunities for the development of inland water transportation. In the year 2000, the State Economic and Trade Commission issued its 'Basic Regulations for Large and Medium-sized State-owned Enterprises to Establish Modern Enterprise System and Tighten up Management (for trial implementation)', formulated for the purposes of driving large and medium-sized state-owned and state-holding enterprises to establish modern enterprise systems and to tighten up management in accordance with its requirements as provided for in the 'Resolution on Certain Key Questions on Reform and Development of SOEs' (adopted in the Fourth Plenary Session of the 15th Central Committee of the Chinese Communist Party). In order to survive the political, social and economic changes taking place in China, restructuring is a long term strategy for COSCO.

Notes

[1] Walder, A.G. (1989) Factory and Manager in an Era of Reform, *The China Quarterly*, 118, 242-64.
[2] Feng, Z. and Zhang, Q. (1993) *Economic Reform and Mechanism Transformation*, Shanxi Economy Press, Shanxi, 129-35.
[3] The land is contracted to peasants through various incentive policies linked to permitting higher levels of commodity production for rural free markets. The reform provided a major incentive to increase private output.
[4] Lee, G. (1994) *Chinese Economic Structure*, Seoul National University Press, Seoul, 6-7.
[5] Liew, L. (1997) *The Chinese Economy in Transition: From Plan to Market*, Edward Elgar Publishing Limited, Cheltenham, 48-9.
[6] Zhong, P. (1994) *Ten-years of Economic Reform: Course, Status Quo, Problem and Future*, Henan People Press, Henan, 78-87.
[7] It endorsed the separation of state ownership from SOEs' management, and government departments at all level would not manage SOEs directly.
[8] The dual-price system applied to three categories of prices: state-set, state-guide (or floating) and free market. Because state-set prices were much lower than the market ones, and most of the products that were subject to state price control were in short supply, enterprises could earn extra profits by shifting their products from state planning to the market. Thus the price of raw materials and other commodities shot up.
[9] Zhong, P. (1994) *op.cit.*, 89-90.
[10] Under this law, state-owned enterprises enjoy 14 decision-making rights, including the rights to decide what to produce, how to invest their funds, and how

to manage and compensate workers. In return, they are held accountable for their performance and can be restructured or go bankrupt.

[11] Tseng, W. (et al.) (1994) *Economic Reform in China: a New Phase*, IMF, Washington DC, 41-5.

[12] Song, J. (1992) Globalisation Strategy of Chinese International Shipping, *Shipping Management*, 1. 3.

[13] The company was better known as Sinochart and was formed along with its sister organisation China National Foreign Transportation, which was better known as Sinotrans, under the Ministry of Foreign Trade. Due to their lack of credit rating on world markets and antagonism of Western powers over the Korea War, Sinochart was forced to operate via Czechoslovakia and Sovfracht until the embargo was lifted in 1958.

[14] Zhang, P. (1995) Loosening Transport Administration and Introducing Foreign Investment in China, *Management World*, 4, 79-9.

[15] Hu, H. (2000) Prospects of China's Shipping 2000, *Proceedings of 2000 China Shipping Seminar*, Beijing, China.

[16] Su, X. (2001) The Opening of Chinese Water Transport Market and Development Trend of its Policies, *Proceedings of 2001 China Shipping Seminar*, February, Beijing, China.

[17] Woodward, P. (1994) Maritime China, *Seatrade Review*, December, 65.

[18] Zhang, J. (1997) Chinese Shipping Moves into Transition, *Lloyd's Shipping Economist*, August, 20.

[19] *Fairplay* (1998) Shipping Exchange Expands, December 3, 36-37.

[20] Wang, R. (1997) Chinese Shipbuilders Going Full Speed Ahead, *Zhong Go Maritime Magazine*, 10-11.

[21] Every month the Ministry of Foreign Trade and Economic Cooperation would meet the MOC and haggle over the space on COSCO's ships. Because the freight rates were mostly fixed, the only real negotiations were over space and ship departure times. The system had guaranteed COSCO steady profits, and the company used them to pay off loans it took out from the country's two banks: the Bank of China, which operated primarily overseas, and the People's Bank, which served as central bank and sole commercial bank for the entire country.

[22] COSCO Shenzhen and Xiamen were established in February and October 1993 respectively.

[23] Brevetti, F. (1997) Breaking Growth to Ease, *Seatrade Review*, November, 55-7.

[24] McElroy, D. (1998) Cosco Container Looks to Maersk as Model, *Seatrade Review*, February, 24.

[25] Flynn, M. (1999) PRC Maritime and the Asian Financial Crisis, *Maritime Policy and Management*, 26, 4, 337-347.

[26] *Seatrade Review* (1996) Shipowner With a Licence to Expand, June, 9.

[27] Wu, H.J. and Nash, C. (2000) Railway Reform in China, *Transport Reviews*, 20, 1, 25-48.

8 Chinese-Polish Co-operation in Liner Shipping

Michael Roe
Institute of Marine Studies
University of Plymouth, United Kingdom

Introduction

Co-operation between China and Poland in the liner trades has been going on since the early 1950s and represents a unique collaboration in shipping that started soon after the Communist regime in Poland came to power. This paper traces the early developments of the collaboration and then goes on to look at the current state of play in the market and the focus of the Chinese-Polish Joint Stock Company 'Chipolbrok', following the economically difficult period of transition in Poland since 1989.

The Early Years Under Communism

The liner service in operation between Poland and China represents one of the earliest known collaborations between state shipping companies over such a long distance. Its creation was a consequence of political agreements between Poland and China, but perhaps more importantly it was a result of the Soviet Union's insistence that an arms shipment shipping service should be developed to supply:

> ...Communist China's armies with East European and Soviet weapons during the Korean War (Harbron, 1962).

Initially called the Gdynia-Takubar Line in the Polish press, it was renamed the Chinese-Polish Shipbroker's Company Limited in 1951 and formally established in June of that year to provide a new liner service to China's ports from the new Polish People's Republic. The company was owned 50-50 by the Chinese Ministry of Communication and the Polish Ministry of Transport and Maritime Economy (Jaszowski, 1992). The company's head office was based in Tientsin, China, with a branch office in Gdynia, Poland and a sub-office in Whampoa in China. The first Polish vessel to operate the route actually did so arriving on the 1st October 1950 – the MV 'Warta'– as part of a Polish Ocean Lines service and following its success, the new Polish-Chinese collaborative company was set up (Polish Maritime News, 1961). In 1951, Polish ships carried around 300,000 tons of freight on the new service, a figure that was to grow to over 770,000 tons by 1953 (Polish Press Agency, 1959).

Officially, the service was sold as one to meet the growing commercial needs of China and the new company began to operate in conjunction with that of Polish Ocean Lines, using chartered tonnage. The Polish authorities were also attempting to take a more aggressive role as shipping operators from Eastern Europe and to move in and dominate the once western dominated Chinese trade to and from Europe.

From its earliest days it was promoted as a most prestigious route, characterised in particular by the fact that payment for services was commonly in hard currency rather than barter (Harbron, 1962), although also common was that currency only formed part of payments. This latter arrangement was particularly appealing to the East Europeans as they:

> ....were willing to pay higher than market rates. They would pay, for instance, US$100 if they only had to pay US$50 in hard currency. This was better than the market rate of US$60 all in hard currency. The rest could be paid by clearing, i.e. a mixture of barter and local currency (Bascombe and Crichton, 1994).

Since its inauguration and up to the early 1960s, it remained foremost in Poland's sea-borne trade plans and to give some idea of its importance, in 1958 some 30 per cent of Polish ocean trade was transported on this route. In addition, by the end of the 1950s nearly all new commissioned passenger-liners of 10,000 dwt were assigned to this trade.

These new vessels had followed the Polish government's largest single purchase of second-hand vessels in December 1951 solely for use on the run to and from China. These three vessels were joined by a number of 'lease-lend' tankers, acquired from the USA to carry jet fuel for the Chinese air force. In total, the number of ships in the early 1950s, working the Polish-Chinese route rose to 15, amounting to a tonnage of 100,000 dead weight.

By December 1951, the route had been renamed again as the Polish China Line or the Tientsin-Gdynia Line. Its significance in the months leading up to this change was clear following the statement quoted by Harbron (1962) and given by Polish Ministry for Foreign Trade, Tadeusz Gede in September of that year in Tientsin:

> During the first seven months of 1951, Polish-Chinese trade rose three times in volume compared with the same period in 1950....Our country receives valuable products for our national economy from the Chinese People's Republic – ores, mining products, vegetable fats, silk....In exchange, Poland sends steel, machines, leather goods, chemicals, textiles and sugar... (Wiadmosci Statystyczna, 1951).

Harbron (1962) emphasised the large number of high-powered delegations that visited Poland from China throughout the 1950s following their first visit in January 1952. Poland was allocated a monopoly of carriage for all goods transported from the CMEA bloc to China, a privilege that was sustained through the decade despite the growth of Chinese maritime power and the creation of new Czech and East German ocean fleets.

During its first year of operation, Chipolbrok recorded 18 sailings, shipping around 140,000 tons of cargo for a total turnaround distance of 1.84 million ton/nautical miles.

By July 1952, there was evidence of increased variety and quantity in Polish trade with China (Trybuna Ludu, 1952). Table 8.1 provides some details.

Table 8.1: China-Poland Trade 1950-1957

	1950	1952	1953	1954	1955	1956	1957
Imports from China	25	95	124	148	139	201	179
Exports to China	9	135	109	118	141	141	149
Total	34	230	233	266	280	342	328

Source: Handel Zagrianiczny (1956, 1957) and Trybuna Ludu (1958), as quoted in Harbron (1962).

Imports from China were dominated by grain, tea, tobacco, textiles, asbestos and ores whilst Polish exports included rolling stock, engines, chemicals and paper products.

From 1954, and the ending of the Korean conflict before then, the service became one of a purely commercial nature characterised by the unusual situation of payment in at least some hard currency by the Chinese to the Polish authorities. The result was often disputes over payments as the Chinese were anxious to minimise these whenever possible to conserve their limited supplies of convertible currency. One agreement was that all goods provided by Poland were to be available at cost price – estimated by Harbron (1962) at 20-30 per cent below market prices – although disputes over actual payments continued throughout the 1950s. Harbron went on to quote Warsaw Radio which on 27th May 1957, announced a net profit of US$2312,000 from the maiden voyage of the 'Marceli Nowotko' between Poland and China.

In 1958 Chinese services in Polish ports were separated so that the port of Gdansk became the base port and Gdynia retained responsibility only for a limited range of imports. The Wladyslaw IV Basin was chosen as the base location in Gdansk because there was adequate room for the frequent movement of heavy-lift and large sized freight. Table 8.2 gives some detail of freight passing through Gdansk and Gdynia on the China line in 1959 and 1960.

Table 8.2: Some Freight Data for the China Line 1959-1960

	1959	1960
Gdansk Imports	36,000	42,000
Gdansk Exports	189,000	164.000
Gdansk Total	**225,000**	**206,000**
Gdynia Imports	-	80,000
Gdynia Exports	-	-
Gdynia Total	-	**80,000**

Source: Polish Maritime News (1961b).

In Gdynia, the handling basin was that of Bojownikow o Pokoj Quay where on average, in 1960, some two vessels a month called. Imports to Poland at this time were typified by latex, rice, cotton, calcium, semi-precious metals, pig iron, textiles and foodstuffs. Exports focussed upon machines, factory plant, pipes, locomotives, excavators, chemicals and precision instruments.

Around this time Chipolbrok took over complete responsibility for the service using their own vessels but when there was a shortage in tonnage, Polish Ocean Lines provided additional capacity. Ships served Gdynia and/or Gdansk and then Wampoa and Tsankong in China, Haiphong in Vietnam and Nampo in North Korea plus additional port visits when necessary en route in Europe or the Far East.

The Chinese-Polish service was examined in some detail in 1961 in terms of port services when it was announced that efficiency in loading/unloading was well above that of the average and was at a rate of 1,000-1,200 tons of general cargo per day. This was considered especially good as the types of cargo were often complex and difficult to handle requiring special care and attention (Polish Maritime News, 1961b). Examples were provided of the 'Przyjazn Narodow' which loaded 9,000 tons of cargo in late 1960 – in 66 hours shorter than expected; the 'Warszawa' loaded 3,300 tons of general cargo in February 1961 in 12 hours less than planned; whilst the 'Moniuszko' loaded 3,500 tons and left port 28 hours earlier than expected. An agreement between the state authorities had been made to apply special fines on vessels of this service for delays and bonuses for speedy despatch.

By 1961, Chipolbrok had 19 vessels on long-term time charter from the main state liner carrier Polish Ocean Lines, operating on the Poland-China service. Typically, cargoes from these two countries dominated the route but increasingly cargoes from Czechoslovakia, DDR, Hungary, Bulgaria, Romania, Vietnam and North Korea featured as well. Ports served were those in Poland and China as ever but now also ports in DDR, Scandinavia, various other West European countries, Vietnam and North Korea. Some vessels also made occasional calls at a variety of Mediterranean and Black Sea ports as well as others en route between the two continents as demand required. The vessels involved were universally modern for the time, often with cooled and frozen holds suited to meat, fruit and other foodstuffs (Polish Maritime News, 1961a).

It was late in 1962 also, that Chipolbrok transferred head office from Tientsin to Shanghai to be central to the Chinese port and shipping industries and they also opened a branch office in Peking. However 1962 was not an easy year for the company and for the first time a decline in trade was recorded. Annual cargo reached only 90 per cent, revenue 87 per cent and shipping profit 20 per cent of targets set.

Things improved in 1963 when the volume of cargo reached 97 per cent of target, revenue was 104 per cent and profit an excellent 270 per cent (showing a true financial profit for the first time since the company's formation). From 1964-1978, production, finance and annual profit targets were exceeded by an average of over 20 per cent. Meanwhile fleet renewal during this period included the introduction of 13 new vessels replacing 12 ageing ones (Quanyuan, 1991).

The company was once again renamed in 1977 to the Chinese-Polish Joint-Stock Shipping Company and soon after this the company bought the first ocean-going vessel in the 10,000 dwt class constructed in a Chinese shipyard (Dajing, 1983).

By 1983, the company owned 21 ocean-going vessels of more than 10,000 dwt aggregating 307,000 dwt. Six were fitted with automated engine rooms, nine with reefer space and 11 with bulk oil tanks. The annual cargo of the line by 1983 totalled 800,000 tons with an average vessel age of 10 years and speed of 16.1 knots. By 1984 the fleet had grown to 350,000 dwt and the cargo carried to over 1 million tons (Maritime China, 1984, Manecki, 1986).

Table 8.3 gives an indication of the growth of the Chipolbrok fleet over the entire period between its formation in 1951, the fall of communism in Poland in 1989 and up to the present day.

Table 8.3: Chipolbrok Fleet, 1951-2001

	Number of Ships	DWT
1951	9	91,120
1952	10	100,690
1953	11	109,710
1954	12	120,835
1955	13	130,632
1956	13	130,421
1957	16	166,392
1958	17	176,668
1959	16	166,630
1960	18	190,638
1961	18	188,341
1962	20	209,141
1963	19	202,891
1964	19	202,891
1965	19	202,891
1966	19	202,891
1967	19	202,891
1968	17	182,049
1969	16	172,244
1970	14	152,786
1971	16	177,635
1972	16	184,729
1973	15	176,319
1974	17	204,326

Table 8.3: concluded

1975	18	219,416
1976	18	219,416
1977	20	250,906
1978	21	264,626
1979	21	271,950
1980	20	262,354
1981	20	264,523
1982	21	291.775
1983	23	328,475
1984	24	346,003
1985	23	351,005
1986	23	375,860
1987	21	358,119
1988	21	369,714
1989	23	405,932
1990	21	374,562
1991	19	361,926
1992	-	-
1993	-	-
1994	21	420,000
1995	21	420,000
1996	21	420,000
1997	-	-
1998	-	-
1999	-	-
2000	20	426,597
2001	20	426,597

Source: Chipolbrok.

The Later Years from 1988

By 1988 the Chinese-Polish Joint Stock Shipping Company had existed through 37 years of Communist control in Poland and China. The company retained its headquarters in Shanghai (China) with a branch office in Gdynia but by 1988 had grown to a fleet size of 21 vessels with 50 per cent of the fleet flying the Polish and 50 per cent the Chinese flag. At this time Chipolbrok actually operated the two biggest ships in the Polish flagged fleet – 'Praca' and 'Pokoj' –whilst the whole fleet had an average age of 10 years; substantially less than the rest of the Polish flagged fleet. By the end of 1988 in total, the company had handled nearly 27 million tonnes of cargo with a turnover of nearly 360 bn tonnes/nautical miles.

The organisation of the company was not typical of East European shipping in general nor of Polish or Chinese shipping in particular. Around 20 Polish employees were permanently retained in Shanghai on a rotation basis whilst the same number of Chinese were to be found in Gdynia. All posts were duplicated – in other words there were two managing directors, two technical directors etc, one each Chinese and Polish. The Branch Office in Gdynia was responsible for all activities at the Polish end of the route in addition to all navigational issues in Europe as far as the Suez Canal.

Chipolbrok's main activity remained operation of the Gdynia – Shanghai line on which a predominance of Polish, Czechoslovak and Hungarian goods were carried from Europe. On return trips from China, a number of West European ports were also incorporated in the schedules.

Chipolbrok's activities had continuously increased during the 1960s and 1970s despite the repeated economic and political problems facing Poland (Polish Maritime News, 1987). As a result their fleet had expanded, and in 1987 the state-owned shipyard in Shanghai was building four new 15,800 dwt multi-purpose vessels for the company. Two 25 year old vessels were planned to be withdrawn (Polish Maritime News, 1988). Plans also existed for four more 20,000 dwt multi-purpose vessels to be constructed in Szczecin.

By 1989 the trade between the two countries had continued to increase (Dajing, 1988, Maritime China, 1988, Polish Maritime News, 1989b). Over 1 million tonnes of cargo was shipped in both 1988 and 1989 between the two countries, largely by Chipolbrok although some was also transported by COSCO (China Ocean Shipping Co.). As a result of the growth Chipolbrok signed a contract with the Yugoslav shipyard of May 3 to build four multi-purpose ships each with a capacity of 1,000 TEU to be delivered between 1991 and 1992 (Maritime China, 1989).

The increase in trade caused some problems however – in particular an increase in damage to cargo and an increasing need to transmit documents between partners more quickly and efficiently. Closer co-operation was thus deemed necessary.

The basis for these developments was the agreement signed between the Polish Office for Maritime Economy and the Chinese Ministry of Communication in 1987. A first result of this agreement was the visit by COSTACO (China Ocean Shipping Tally Co.) to Poland which was followed by a return visit to China by the Polish state company Shipcontrol. Both companies specialised in cargo inspection. An agreement was signed by the two companies to improve data and administration exchange and cargo carriage standards. Further collaboration was also to continue through ship design and technical co-operation with specific reference to new vessels for Chipolbrok (Polish Maritime News, 1989a).

The year 1988 was also a year of success for the company as the difficulties of the previous decade were overcome. Some 108 voyages were completed and 1.141 million tonnes of cargo carried, representing 109 per cent and 114.1 per cent respectively of the year's targets. Both income and profits were larger than projected.

By 1989 the fleet size was 23 vessels with an average age of only 8.8 years. In the previous five years the annual average total cargo shifted had been over 1 million tonnes and fixed assets were calculated as '...nine times the initial investment' (Quanyuan, 1990).

Late 1989 and early 1990 figures were very much poorer as the initial effects of the changes in Poland began to bite. In particular business between China and Poland and Czechoslovakia declined substantially and competition for cargo thus increased greatly. The last quarter of 1989, traditionally the peak of the year in terms of cargo revenue, represented only 13.64 per cent of the year's profit. Ships sailing from Poland suffered the most.

The extent of the traditional freight decline was typified by China-Poland cargoes which reduced from 200,000 tons annually to 20,000 tons in 1989 and China-Poland cargoes from 500,000 tons to 50,000 tons the same year.

As a result, Chipolbrok took a number of steps:

• Strengthened management and improved quality of service. This resulted in an improvement in the cargo safety record so that defrayments for cargo loss and damage reduced to 49 per cent of the previous year.

• Increased cargo canvassing and strict adherence to schedules. This particularly involved acquiring cargo from locations other than Poland and China located en route between origin and destination. Cargo sources were also enlarged by co-operating closer with Sinotrans (state forwarders) in China.

• New liner services. Although the shipment of conventional cargo had declined drastically, the figures for 1989 showed that Chipolbrok carried 14,285 TEU, which was an increase of 123 per cent over 1988. The company by then had nearly 2,000 new containers available and with better management, far fewer empties were carried. The container operations had only really begun in late 1987 (although containerised tractors were first carried in 1977) and as a result it had been anticipated that there would be some bedding in to be done.

- Financial regulations and economies. Both financial regulation and business accounting were tightened. Bunkering was now always undertaken where fuel costs were lowest as were ship repairs.
- Crew discipline. Rules were tightened as well.
- Logistics. New market opportunities in Eastern Europe remained difficult to grasp but it was hoped with new logistic principles installed, this would improve.

The immediate impact was apparent in that during 1990, Chipolbrok carried a respectable 1.374 million tonnes of cargo on 116 sailings – an increase of 18 sailings and 230,000 tonnes on the previous year.

In 1991, Chipolbrok celebrated its 40th year. By then it operated 19 modern, multi-purpose ocean-going vessels totalling over 360,000 dwt with a capacity of approximately 11,000 TEU. Many of these vessels also had reefer capabilities and deep tanks for bulk liquid cargoes. Traditional loading ports in Europe remained Gdynia, Helsingborg, Hamburg, Rotterdam, Antwerp and various ports in the Black Sea and the Mediterranean. Ports in the Far East regularly included the major locations in Taiwan, Korea, Japan and China. Three new vessels of 22,000 dwt (1,015 TEU) were to be delivered in 1992 (Siemaszko, 1991).

By 1991, the division of total freight revenue origin was 70 per cent from China, 10-15 per cent from Poland, and 8-10 per cent from other East European countries and other freight providers en route. The Chinese market was dominated by machines, vehicles, heavy-lift equipment and factory equipment. However, the Chinese share of the westbound freight declined in volume in 1990 to only 31 per cent of the total, a trend which was evidently continuing during the first half of 1991 (Table 8.4). Goods from Eastern Europe were dominated by steel (44 per cent), fertilisers and other bulk cargoes (21 per cent), machinery (8 per cent), soda (5 per cent), PVC (3 per cent), spare parts (2 per cent) and other items (17 per cent). Around 40 per cent of all cargoes were now containerised.

Chipolbrok remained an 'outsider' in the liner trade and as a result, the combination of low rates at the time and the effective control of much of the market by highly specialised carriers and cartels (conferences) meant that their vessels were competing only for low value (low revenue) bulk cargoes on the general market and for the increasingly limited number of better paid Chinese managed cargoes which were increasingly being directed to COSCO – the Chinese state owned operator. To overcome immediate problems stemming in part from the new trade agreement between the Polish and Chinese governments in 1989 that all trade would be conducted in foreign (hard) currency, there was talk of new arrangements of payments involving the 'mutual balance of purchases expressed in domestic currencies' although it is unclear how far these discussions went (Polish Maritime News, 1989b).

Table 8.4: Cargo Ownership, Chipolbrok Westbound Freight 1991 (1st Half)

Cargo Owners	Freight (million tons)	%
China	103,655	17.4
Poland	98,329	16.5
Czechoslovakia	23,455	3.9
Hungary	2,359	0.4
Bulgaria	1,367	0.2
Morocco	15,206	2.6
General Market	351,016	59.0

Source: Siemaszko, 1991.

Plans also existed to extend port coverage to Aqaba (Jordan), Jeddah (Saudi Arabia), Jakarta and Surabaya (Indonesia) in addition to the existing Poland-China run. Monthly sailings were planned along with other developments involving Libya, Sri Lanka and Singapore.

Table 8.5: Cargo Ownership, Chipolbrok Eastbound Freight 1991 (1st Half)

Cargo Owners	Freight (million tons)	%
Eastern Europe (including Poland)	17,821 (4,291)	6.1 (1.5)
China CIF	77,059	26.3
Morocco	15,206	5.2
General Market	182,737	62.4

Source: Siemaszko, 1991.

In recognition of the difficult times in the early 1990s and the delivery of four new ships from Croatian shipyards in 1992, a number of vessels were time chartered to Rickmers Lines. In June of the same year a new service between Poland and the USA began continuing to China through the Panama Canal (Lloyds Ship Manager, 1992).

The changed approach to the markets by diversifying into serving many other ports between China and Poland was the salvation of Chipolbrok at a very difficult time. By 1993, only a small proportion of traffic was associated with the old China-Poland trade and 16,000 TEU were carried that year, a rise of 25 per cent over the numbers carried before the diversification in port calls (Bascombe and Chrichton, 1994). Liner services offered are shown in Table 8.6.

Table 8.6: Chipolbrok Liner Services, 1994

Route	Frequency	Ports of Call
Asia/Europe	4 sailings monthly	Dalian, Xingang, Qingdao, Shanghai, Hong Kong, Singapore, Casablanca (monthly), Antwerp, Rotterdam, Hamburg, Gdynia
Europe/Asia	2 sailings monthly	Gdynia, Hamburg, Antwerp, Shanghai, Xingang, Qingdao, Dalian
Europe/Red Sea/Asia	Monthly	Gdynia, Hamburg, Antwerp, Aqaba, Jeddah, Singapore, Huangpu, Dalian
Italy/Asia	2 sailings monthly	Genoa, Oristano, Venice, Hong Kong/Huangpu, Shanghai, Xingang, Qingdao

Source: Adapted from Bascombe and Crichton, 1994.

Some 21 vessels were now operated with a capacity of 13,300 TEU and to reflect the growth in the company, plans were made by the two state's ministries to invest in 800 x 20ft and 1,500 x 40ft new dry containers. Also planned was the purchase of two second-hand vessels from a German owner of approximately 670 TEU. In addition to four planned new vessel investments this would turn a state controlled semi-liner company into a state-owned but privately orientated, fully-liner organisation operating entirely in the commercial market-place. As Andrzej Karnabal, managing director of Chipolbrok Poland said:

> The transformation has been performed without financial losses to the company and 1993 was closed with good profit. The first quarter of 1994 was also successful, therefore the management of Chipolbrok is rather optimistic regarding the future of the company (Bascombe and Crichton, 1994).

In 1995 total freight carried was 1.4 million tonnes and 220,000 TEU on the 21 vessels owned by the company (Berenyi, 1995; Lloyds Ship Manager, 1996). Average age of these vessels was 10 years, of which eight ships sailed under the Chinese flag, nine under the Polish and four under the Cypriot. Some 420 seafarers were employed divided between 11 vessels with Polish staff and 10 vessels with Chinese. Chipolbrok provided three sailings a month from Polish and North European ports to China – one via Red Sea ports, in addition to another from the Mediterranean and four sailings a month from the main ports of China to Europe.

By the year 2000 Chipolbrok's fleet comprised 20 vessels with a combined capacity of more than 426,000 dwt, each geared multi-purpose ships built between 1977 and 1998. Their freight capacity varied between 16,000 dwt and 28,000 dwt with container capacity between 320 and 1,100 TEU. By then six vessels were Chinese flagged, nine Cypriot and five Maltese. None were flagged with Poland. Smaller vessels were normally used between the Mediterranean and China, the bigger serving Northern Europe. Nearly all types of cargo could be carried from containers to liquid bulk giving the company flexibility in a market that changed regularly.

The main Chinese ports remained the major markets – Shanghai, Huangpu, Xingang, Qingdao and Dalian – whilst from Europe, Antwerp was responsible for 25 per cent of all cargo of which 60-70 per cent was for China. Some 100,000 tonnes of cargo moved annually between China and Antwerp. In Northern Europe the only regular ports of call were Antwerp and Hamburg although ports in the Baltic were commonly visited for commodities such as steel (Vandevoorde, 2000). During 2000, Chipolbrok shipped over 700,000 tonnes of cargo (Ahlers, 2001).

In 2001 Chipolbrok acquired a stake (73 per cent) in Baltic Container Lines (BCL) taking the majority shareholding along with Polish Ocean Lines (POL) (18 per cent) and C. Hartwig Forwarders (9 per cent). BCL had been set up by the Port of Gdynia with POL and Hartwig a number of years before to develop the container feeder industry to the Port of Gdynia (Lloyds List, 2000). Meanwhile in February 2001, Chipolbrok began a regular service between Bilbao (Spain) and the main ports of China, Indonesia and Korea as part of their North European – China service (Lloyds List, 2001).

By mid 2001, the year of the company's 50th anniversary, the market scenario for Chipolbrok was about to change again with the impending entry of China to the World Trade Organisation (WTO). The existing 50-50 ownership by the two states was not suited to the requirements of the WTO and consequently there would be the need to expand ownership and allow other investors to come in if they wished. The transformation to a new competitive and open environment was not expected to be quick but was inevitable (China Daily, 2001).

The company by now had over 50 agencies in Europe and the Far East and also representative offices in Beijing, Guangzhou, Tianjin and Hong Kong (China), and in Hamburg (Germany). In China, Chipolbrok owned the China-Poland International Forwarding Company, the Shanghai-Gdynia International Transportation Agency Co. Ltd and a container depot in Shanghai. In Poland it retained its main shareholding in BCL. Chipolbrok had also set up a joint venture with Singapore based Chipobal Shipping Pty Ltd and a Dutch partner Sinepol Shipping and Agency b.v. Rotterdam. In addition it had shares in COSCO Poland and the Polish-Belarussian forwarding agent Mirtrans.

Chipolbrok carried out several on-shore development projects including housing, office and leisure/sports facilities. Since 1999, the company has been certified by Lloyds Register of Shipping as ISO9002 and ISM Code compliant (*The Coastal Times*, 2001).

Conclusions

Chipolbrok has migrated from a collaborative state venture, set up purely for political reasons in the early 1950s to a fully commercial activity by the turn of the century, generally highly profitable and although still state owned, increasingly pushed towards becoming more private sector orientated and with the influence of WTO membership for China since 2001, having to adapt to new pressures and influences. A unique company in its structure and success, its markets have diversified as transition has progressed both in East Europe and China and its ability to survive through the 1950s to the new millennium is largely a consequence of its inherent flexibility.

References

Ahlers (2001) Chipolbrok Plans New Vessels With Heavy-lift Capacity, *Ahlers Newsletter*, May 23, http://ahlers.com.
Bascombe, A. and Crichton, J. (1994) Changing Philosophies, *Containerisation International*, October, 66-67.

Berenyi, I. (1995) Emerging From the Gloom, *Seatrade Review*, December, 73-75.

China Daily (2001) June 14 (http://www.xinhuanet.com).

Dajing, Y. (1983) Chipolbrok in 33rd Year, *Maritime China*, 1, 1, 55-57.

Dajing, Y. (1988) Chipolbrok – Expansion Plans, *Maritime China*, 4, 4, 71.

Handel Zagrianiczny (1956) no. 11.

Handel Zagrianiczny (1957) no. 4.

Harbron, J.D. (1962) *Communist Ships and Shipping*, Adlard Coles; London.

Jaszowski, J. (1992) The Crisis in Polish Shipping, *Schiff und Hafen*, 9, 34-37.

Lloyds List (2000) Port of Gdynia Nears End of Restructuring, September 1.

Lloyds List (2001) Bilbao Raises Outer Abra Stakes, February 20.

Lloyds Ship Manager (1992) Chipolbrok Secure, August, 35.

Lloyds Ship Manager (1996) Joint Venture Copes With Change, August, 29.

Manecki, A. (1986) Zur Baltexpo '86: Chinesisch-Polnische Schiffsgesellschaft S.A. Chipolbrok, *Schiff und Hafen*, 3, 16-17.

Maritime China (1984) Chipolbrok to Order More Ships? *Maritime China*, 2, 2, 53-54.

Maritime China (1988) West German Links with China, *Maritime China*, 4, 4, 95.

Maritime China (1989) Chipolbrok Modernises its Fleet, *Maritime China*, 7, 1, 95.

Polish Maritime News (1961a) China Line at Gdansk, 35/36, 3-4.

Polish Maritime News (1961b) Shipping Co-operation with China, 2.

Polish Maritime News (1987) Rejuvenating of Fleet, 10, 6-7.

Polish Maritime News (1988) Chipolbrok's Fleet, 5, 2.

Polish Maritime News (1989a) Co-operation with Chinese Shippers, 7/8, 2.

Polish Maritime News (1989b) Shipping between China and Poland is Increasing, 3, 18.

Polish Press Agency (1959) Sino-Polish Relations, *Weekly Review*, 29th September, 5.

Quanyuan, S. (1990) Chipolbrok's Achievements, *Maritime China*, 8, 2, 65-66.

Quanyuan, S. (1991) Chipolbrok Success Story, *Maritime China*, 9, 3, 53-56.

Siemaszko, R. (1991) Chipolbrok's Orientation, *Polish Maritime Industry Journal*, 2, November, 7-9.

The Coastal Times (2001) The Chinese-Polish Joint Stock Shipping Company Chipolbrok, September, 43.

Trybuna Ludu (1958) November 15.

Trybuna Ludu (1952) July 12.

Vandevoorde, J. (2000) Chipolbrok Sees Imports Growing, *Lloyds Special Report.*

Wiadmosci Statystyczna (1951) *Statistical Bulletin, Official Publication of the Main Statistical Office*, Warsaw, July-August.

9 Sino-Korean Maritime Co-operation

Young-Tae Chang
Korea Maritime Institute
Seoul, Korea

Introduction

Maritime co-operation between China and Korea has a long history that dates back more than a thousand years when ancient Korea commenced trade with ancient China through Shandong Province via the Yellow Sea route. China has been the closest ally in terms of both technology and culture, with Korea from 1945 until the present day. Following the dormant period of 1945 to 1979, China commenced an 'open door policy', which reactivated maritime co-operation. This co-operation was in particular propelled by the epoch-making establishment of diplomatic ties between China and Korea in August 1992 and strengthened further by a series of maritime talks and the signing of a maritime agreement on May 27th 1993 and its entry into force on June 28th that year.

Thus far the maritime co-operation between China and Korea has been very successful, generating numerous unprecedented records in the growth rates of trade volumes, cargo volumes, shipping lines and routes. For instance, the trade volume between the two countries skyrocketed from 19 million US$ in 1979 to 22.552 billion US$ in 1999 representing an annual growth rate of 43 per cent. China was the fourth biggest trade partner to Korea and Korea ranked the fifth for China at the end of 1999 if the EU is considered as a single entity.[1] The seaborne cargo volume has been growing at an accelerating speed since the 'Melisa's' maiden voyage between the two countries in 1989. Container cargoes and numbers of shipping routes more vividly reflect rapid growth. At present, there are 28 container vessels and seven ferries in operation solely on the Yellow Sea. It appears to be agreed between both countries that maritime co-operation has been mutually beneficial and thus its furtherance is aspired to for the future.

---

[1] Yang, J. and Kim, H. (2000)

In spite of the successful co-operation hitherto, it is not enough to be complacent and let everything remain as it is, since certain areas appear to still exist that need to be supplemented for the future. The main objective of this paper is to review maritime co-operation between China and Korea and identify the current issues.

The next section considers economic co-operation and the transport network system in Northeast Asia before examining the details of current issues between China and Korea in the maritime field.

Economic Co-operation and the Transport Network in Northeast Asia

Like the bloc economy movements of the European Union and NAFTA, the Northeast Asian[2] region is increasingly discussing the need for regional co-operation. The economic importance of the region in the world is rather significant. The Northeast Asian economies' share in world merchant trade were 18.1 per cent and 14.5 per cent of world exports and imports, respectively in 1998. Three Northeast Asian countries – Japan, China and Korea – account for approximately 12.9 per cent (US$ 704 billion) of total world exports and about 9.2 per cent (US$515 billion) of total world imports. Their intra-regional trade (exports and imports between them) share is about 9-31 per cent of each country's total exports or imports.[3]

Since the early 1970s the rapid growth of economies in the Northeast Asian region has been accompanied and stimulated by the establishment of a supra-regional transport network. Hubs occupy a key position within the networks, offering a variety of opportunities for global and regional marketing facilitated by frequent services and comparatively low distribution costs. During the 1980s, Tokyo emerged as a global, multi-modal network hub on a par with London and New York. At a regional level, Hong Kong and Singapore have battled for the right to become the single network hub in the Asia-Pacific region.[4]

In recognition of the importance of infrastructure, all countries in the region have been developing their transport network systems to become major logistic centres of Northeast Asia one way or another. For instance, major ports of Japan appear ready to become the regional hubs and the comparatively few ports of Korea, such as Pusan, Kwangyang, Inchon and

[2]In this paper, Northeast Asia denotes Japan, China, Korea, Taiwan and Hong Kong.
[3]Nam, S. (2000).
[4]Rimmer, P.J. (1993).

Pyoungtaek (new port), are on the way to hub status. Likewise, China, Russia and North Korea are rushing to take the initiative in the Tumen River Project, whereby they can develop a strongly emerging logistical centre in the region through port and inland transport developments as well as the accommodation of a free industrialised zone. Upon completion of the project, this area is expected to function as an 'economic corridor'[5] in this region. In line with this development, Russia and China have already developed a series of trans-continental railway networks in order to meet the demand for cargoes between Europe and Asia and as part of the plan of the two Koreas through the reconnection of Korean railways[6] to reconstruct railway linkages.

Thus far, all the tramp shipping routes that have been established in the region and container routes are either in active operation between Japan, China and Korea, or at a developing stage between China, Russia, Japan and Korea. Only container routes to and from North Korea are, at present, under-developed; however, they are likely to be opened sooner or later.

As for the trans-continental railways, it is noteworthy that since the inception of services in 1972 handling 2,000 TEU, the Trans Siberian Railway (TSR) once carried 138,000 TEU in 1983 then declined severely to 8,000 TEU in 1998 but bounced back to 25,000 TEU in 1999 (MOMAF). The decline was caused by a range of unsettling factors after the collapse of the former Soviet Union, and the frequent delay to cargoes (for instance, it was common to have 1 to 2 week delay). The Trans Chinese Railway (TCR) with the Trans Manchuria Railway (TMR) and the Trans Mongolian Railway (TMGR) started competition with the TSR from the mid-1990s in transporting cargoes between Europe and Asia.[7] The two Koreas are also planning to gain access to the TSR and the TCR via a reconnection of North and South Korea railways – that is the TKR (Trans Korea Railway).[8]

---

[5] This concept was developed by Professor Peter J. Rimmer of Australian National University and means in general, the most economically central area of the region.

[6] The two Koreas agreed in the accord of South-North exchanges and cooperation, taking effect on February 19, 1992 (Chapter III, Article 19) that the two sides shall reconnect railroads and roads that have been cut off and shall open South-North sea and air transport routes (*Korea Herald,* February 20, 1992). Then, while exploring cooperation again recently during the Kim Dae-Jung regime, September 18, in 2000 witnessed a ground-breaking ceremony to rejoin the disconnected railway between South Korea and North Korea. This construction for the disconnected part was planned to be completed by September 2001 although this has so far failed to occur and the eventual connection with the TSR and TCR will be completed by 2005.

[7] TCR very often includes TMR and TMGR.

[8] On completion of the TKR, two lines in Korea are connected to transcontinental railways. The first line along the west coast of Korea – Kyoung-Ui-Sun (Seoul-Sinuiju-Line) – can be connected with the TMR. The second line along the east coast

Therefore, it is expected that regarding transcontinental cargoes, there will be competition between six alternatives, namely, the existing sea route, TSR, TCR, TMR, TMGR and TKR. In that case, the transportation capability connecting Europe and Asia as well as the Pacific Ocean will be strengthened. This will increase transport efficiency[9] by attracting the world's attention and help Northeast Asia play a key role in the Asia Pacific region and the world's other regional economic zones (Jon, 1992).

To sum up, future trade and investment prospects will be strongly influenced by the evolution of the pattern of trade specialisation among the Northeast Asian economies and the policy framework in which those trade and investment flows occur. In this respect, all Northeast Asian countries' willingness to participate in the Tumen River Project implies stronger regional co-operation than ever before and as such, a more efficient transport network in the region can be envisioned in the foreseeable future. This trend will be strengthened further particularly by the two Koreas' co-operation in recent years and also between the Koreas and neighbouring countries.

Current Issues in Sino-Korean Maritime Co-operation

Sino-Korean trade really started in 1979 with a record of 19 million US$ but it had increased to 22.6 billion US$ in 1999 at an annual growth rate of 43 per cent (Table 9.1).

There are some 19 container ship liner routes which operate services between China and Korea, facilitated by 28 container vessels from 20 companies at the end of December, 1999. These companies come from three different groupings – either Korean or Chinese or joint-ventures between the two countries or third party countries. The service is weekly and ports of call are Pusan, Masan, Oolsan and Kwangyang in Korea and Shanghai, Tianjin, Dalian, Qingdao, Yingkou, Lianyungang, Nanjing, Nantong, Zhanjiangang and Ningbo in China. Korean companies call at four major container ports in China – Shanghai, Tianjin, Dalian and Qingdao – and Chinese companies use

– Kyoung-Won-Sun (Seoul-Wonsan-Line) – can be connected either with the TSR or with the TMR.

[9] According to a number of research studies, if Korea utilises the TCR, it can reduce the transportation distance from Pusan to Rotterdam by about 2,147km compared with the TSR with a resultant cut of about 20 per cent in transportation cost. Furthermore, transportation by the TCR will be shorter than the sea route by about 9,152 km (Hong, 1992).

a number of other small ports such as Lianyungang, Yingkou, Nanjing, Nantong, Zhanjiangang and Ningbo in addition to the four major ports to cover sizeable areas of cargo origins and destinations in China and thus provide a better logistical service. Vessel sizes are all in the service range from 178 TEU to 918 TEU, although the majority remain in the range of 400-600 TEU.

Table 9.1: Sino-Korean Trade (million US$)

Year	Total	Imports to Korea	Exports from Korea	Balance
1979	18.8	14.8	4.0	-10.8
1990	2,853	2,268	585	-1,683
1996	19,916	8,539	11,377	2,838
1997	23,689	10,117	13,572	3,455
1998	18,428	6,484	11,944	5,460
1999	22,552	8,867	13,685	4,818

Source: Yang and Kim, KIEP, 2000 and KOTRA.

Sino-Korean container cargoes have increased sharply from 56,252 TEU in 1990 to 925,751 TEU in 1999 at an annual growth rate of 36.5 per cent (Table 9.2). Of the cargo in 1999, 47 per cent was trans-shipment cargo. Import cargo to Korea was more than export cargo from Korea and the trans-shipment amount of the import cargo (308,991 TEU) was more than twice the trans-shipment cargo of export cargo (128,012 TEU). This phenomenon results from the fact that Korean ports are more actively used for outbound Chinese cargoes as trans-shipment ports than inbound Chinese cargoes. Some 86 per cent of total Sino-Korean container cargoes were handled in the four major ports and the order of throughput was Tianjin, Qingdao, Shanghai and Dalian. The trans-shipment cargoes were also in the same order among the four major ports (Table 9.3).

Passengers by ferry service increased from 248,847 persons in 1998 to 402,632 persons in 1999 with what can be described as a remarkable growth rate of 61.8 per cent (Table 9.4).

The first direct sea route between China and Korea was opened in June, 1989 before the establishment of diplomatic ties when a joint-venture, Sinokor was founded and the 'Melisa' was on her maiden voyage. Then shipping companies on the Yellow Sea increased remarkably so that, at present, ten Korean companies, another ten Chinese companies, six joint-ventures and four third-party companies (Table 9.2) are operating in line with the sharp increase of trade and cargoes.

Table 9.2: Container Cargoes, Sino-Korean Routes (TEU)

	Company	1998			1999			Increase (%)
		Exports from Korea	Imports to Korea	Subtotal	Exports from Korea	Imports to Korea	Subtotal	
	SINOKOR	37,596 (9,048)	32,265 (18,605)	69,861 (27,653)	47,646 (10,609)	49,458 (23,286)	97,104 (33,895)	39.00 (22.57)
	Choyang	14,755 (3,603)	19,593 (17,399)	34,348 (21,002)	14,294 (3,444)	20,562 (15,510)	34,856 (18,954)	1.48 (-9.75)
	Dongyoung	11,358 (4,682)	11,087 (5,656)	22,445 (10,338)	13,409 (4,394)	13,883 (4,485)	27,292 (8,879)	21.6 (-14.11)
Alliance Group A	Hanjin	19,789 (9,650)	31,041 (29,144)	50,830 (38,794)	18,461 (8,120)	24,786 (22,557)	43,247 (30,677)	-14.92 (-20.92)
	Namsung	8,060 (671)	4,975 (2,553)	13,035 (3,224)	16,117 (2,370)	19,363 (9,325)	35,480 (11,695)	172.19 (262.75)
	Pan Ocean	11,708 (208)	6,465 (1,871)	18,173 (2,079)	16,343 (1,678)	16,130 (4,579)	32,473 (6,227)	78.69 (199.52)
	Subtotal	*65,670 (18,814)*	*73,161 (56,623)*	*138,831 (75,437)*	*78,624 (20,006)*	*94,724 (56,426)*	*173,348 (76,432)*	*24.86 (1.32)*
	Chonk-young	7,587 (1,204)	6,592 (2,542)	14,179 (3,746)	9,955 (1,500)	11,787 (4,259)	21,742 (5,759)	53.34 (53.74)
Alliance Group B	Hyundai	35,481 (20,263)	49,912 (41,351)	85,393 (61,614)	35,996 (19,406)	56,559 (44,151)	92,555 (63,557)	8.39 (3.15)
	KMTC	13,397 (4,832)	16,781 (13,529)	30,178 (18,361)	18,976 (3,975)	24,282 (17,753)	43,258 (21,728)	43.34 (18.34)
	Tan Continental	7,713 (2,349)	9,760 (4,478)	17,473 (6,827)	9,599 (3,340)	12,926 (4,512)	22,525 (7,852)	28.91 (15.01)
	Subtotal	*64,178 (28,648)*	*83,045 (61,900)*	*147,223 (90,548)*	*74,526 (28,221)*	*105,554 (70,675)*	*180,080 (98,896)*	*22.32 (9.22)*

Table 9.2: continued

	COSCO	18,210 (630)	15,355 (1,211)	33,565 (1,841)	13,386 (1,974)	20,210 (1,298)	33,596 (3,272)	0.09 (77.73)
	China Shipping	15,389 (6,364)	10,084 (5,215)	25,473 (11,579)	14,382 (5,335)	16,590 (8,656)	30,972 (13,991)	21.59 (20.83)
	Shanghai Jinjang	10,309 (4,594)	13,288 (12,140)	23,597 (16,734)	11,911 (6,019)	7,071 (5,967)	18,982 (11,986)	-19.56 (-28.37)
S	Dalian	567 (-)	3,801 (3,768)	4,368 (3,768)	1,365 (611)	3,190 (2,673)	4,555 (3,284)	4.28 (-12.85)
I N	Qin-gdao	5,964 (1,766)	10,794 (8,931)	16,758 (10,697)	7,904 (4,803)	11,225 (8,334)	19,129 (13,137)	14.15 (-12.85)
O	Nan-jing	3,751 (551)	1,198 (769)	4,949 (1,320)	4,463 (653)	1,643 (895)	6,106 (1,548)	23.38 (17.27)
T R	Lianyu-ngang	1,951 (1,144)	5,448 (2,281)	7,399 (3,425)	2,481 (1,103)	4,975 (1,794)	7,456 (2,897)	0.77 (-15.42)
A N	Zhang-jiang	1,855 (528)	1,565 (362)	3,420 (890)	2,903 (871)	2,166 (212)	5,069 (1,083)	48.22 (21.69)
S	*Sub-total*	*10,433 (3,989)*	*22,806 (16,111)*	*36,894 (20,100)*	*19,176 (8,042)*	*23,226 (13,915)*	*42,402 (21,957)*	*14.93 (9.24)*
	CSC	10,433 (1,976)	9,016 (6,740)	19,449 (8,716)	10,140 (4,372)	17,947 (12,138)	28,087 (16,510)	44.41 (89.42)
	Coheung	16,607 (8,233)	43,274 (35,635)	59,881 (43,868)	22,753 (14,490)	75,216 (66,686)	97,969 (81,176)	63.61 (85.05)
	Subtotal	*85,036 (25,786)*	*113,823 (77,052)*	*198,859 (102,838)*	*91,748 (40,232)*	*160,260 (108,660)*	*252,008 (148,892)*	*26.73 (44.78)*

Chinese Shipping Companies

Table 9.2: concluded

Sino-Korea Joint-Ventures	C & K Ferry	6,288 (1,435)	6,112 (2,134)	12,400 (3,569)	7,072 (1,919)	8,625 (1,155)	14,586 (3,074)	17.63 (-13.87)
	Dain Ferry	6,737 (-)	3,903 (-)	10,640 (-)	8,947 (-)	6,046 (-)	14,993 (-)	40.91 (-)
	Jinchon	5,385 (-)	6,196 (293)	11,581 (293)	7,062 (164)	7,059 (164)	14,121 (164)	21.93 (-44.03)
	Weidong	22,825 (-)	16,263 (-)	39,088 (-)	31,172 (-)	24,801 (-)	55,973 (-)	43.20 (-)
	Dandong Ferry	543 (-)	600 (-)	1,143 (-)	3,545 (-)	3,490 (-)	7,035 (-)	51549 (-)
	Shanghai-Inchon	750 (-)	366 (-)	1,116 (-)	4,507 (-)	3,271 (-)	7,778 (-)	59695 (-)
	Subtotal	*42,528 (1,435)*	*33,440 (2,427)*	*75,968 (3,862)*	*62,305 (1,919)*	*52,181 (1,319)*	*114,486 (3,238)*	*50.70 (-16.16)*
Third-Party Companies	New Orient	17,994 (7,524)	16,964 (11,970)	34,958 (19,494)	18,250 (8,062)	17,660 (12,436)	35,910 (20,498)	2.72 (5.15)
	EAS	10,724 (5,054)	22,056 (17,947)	32,780 (23,001)	13,800 (8,776)	26,008 (20,405)	39,808 (29,181)	21.44 (26.87)
	T.M.S.C	12,824 (6,905)	16,563 (12,020)	29,387 (18,925)	12,365 (8,981)	18,237 (15,151)	30,602 (24,132)	4.13 (27.51)
	MAERSK	969 (247)	1,394 (1,314)	2,363 (1,561)	1,717 (1,206)	688 (633)	2,405 (1,839)	1.78 (17.81)
	Subtotal	*42,511 (19,730)*	*56,977 (43,251)*	*99,488 (62,981)*	*46,132 (27,025)*	*62,593 (48,625)*	*108,725 (75,650)*	*9.28 (20.12)*
TOTAL		**337,519 (103,461)**	**392,711 (259,858)**	**730,230 (363,319)**	**400,981 (128,012)**	**524,770 (308,991)**	**925,751 (437,003)**	**26.78 (20.28)**

Source: MOMAF (Korea Ministry of Maritime Affairs and Fisheries).

At present 28 container vessels and seven ferry vessels are in operation on the Yellow Sea. The ferry services are on eight routes provided by seven vessels (Table 9.5). Inchon/Weihai services are most frequent – three times a week and others are once or twice a week. The ferries can carry 110-293 TEU containers in addition to 290-656 passengers per vessel.

In Korea, the total container cargoes were about 7.7 million TEU in 1999. Of these, the Port of Pusan handled 6.44 million TEU representing 85 per cent of the nationwide total volumes and ranking fourth in the world, taking over the place of the Port of Rotterdam. The proportion of Pusan in the national container throughput has been decreasing slightly and this trend is expected to be exacerbated as the Port of Kwangyang (new port) is developed according to its development plan (Table 9.6).

The container cargoes in Pusan are handled by five specialised container terminals with a total annual capacity of 4.15 million TEU. Since the cargoes demanded in Pusan surpassed the total capacity of all the five specialised terminals, conventional piers had to handle 1.1 million TEU to supplement the gap between supply and demand of container port facilities. The characteristics of the five container terminals in Pusan and the other in Kwangyang Port are shown in Table 9.7.

Table 9.3: Container Cargoes by Chinese Port in Sino-Korean Trade (TEU)

Port	Exports from Korea	Imports to Korea	Total
Tianjin	96,636 (40,733)	154,231 (106,702)	**250,867 (147,435)**
Qingdao	86,416 (22,864)	119,044 (65,940)	**205,460 (88,804)**
Shanghai	104,061 (28,019)	92,466 (51,378)	**196,527 (79,397)**
Dalian	52,946 (19,170)	88,353 (56,342)	**141,299 (75,512)**
Others	60,922 (17,226)	70,676 (28,629)	**131,598 (45,855**
Total	**400,981 (128,012)**	**524,770 (308,991)**	**925,751 (437,003)**

Trans-shipment cargo is in brackets ( ).
Source: Author.

The table shows that the three terminals in Pusan can handle about one million TEU respectively, with each terminal accommodating four 50,000 DWT ships. The other two terminals can handle 300-400,000 TEU per terminal. The Jasungdae terminal was developed in two phases as the first specialised container terminal in Korea. It used to be run by a state-owned company before being privatised in September, 1999. The Port of Pusan lacks a container yard area within the terminal and therefore, most of the containers have to be transferred to the 37 Off-Dock Container Yards dispersed in the city. This causes traffic congestion. Pusan plans to develop a new container port (Kaduck New Container Port) in two phases by 2011, with a view to providing 24 berths and having an annual capacity of 4.6 million TEU. Kwangyang has also been developing its second phase plan from 1995 to 2001 in addition to its present terminal. The new development in the second phase will provide four berths for 50,000 dwt vessels and another four berths for 20,000 dwt vessels, resulting in an annual capacity of 1.44 million TEU.

Table 9.4: Passengers Travelling by Sino-Korean Ferry Services

	1998			1999			
	Outbound from Korea	Inbound for Korea	Subtotal	Outbound from Korea	Inbound for Korea	Subtotal	Increase (%)
Inchon/ Weihai	57,199	54,849	112,048	66,190	70,251	136,441	**21.8**
Inchon/ Qingdao	15,825	15,069	30,894	24,251	27,171	51,422	**66.4**
Inchon/ Tianjin	15,258	13,660	28,918	19,404	22,035	41,439	**43.3**
Pusan/ Yantai	4,412	4,105	8,517	7,772	7,681	15,453	**81.4**
Kunsan/ Yantai	3,929	4,292	8,221	8,353	9,115	17,468	**112.5**
Inchon/ Dalian	21,982	10,613	42,595	32,803	35,727	68,530	**60.9**
Inchon/ Dandong	8,966	7,979	16,945	30,406	31,170	61,576	**263.4**
Inchon/ Cheju/ Shanghai	490	219	709	4,991	5,312	10,303	**1,353**
Total	**128,061**	**120,786**	**248,847**	**194,170**	**208,462**	**402,632**	**61.8**

* Source: MOMAF.

China handled 17.7 million TEU in 1999. Of these, Shanghai handled 4.2 million TEU and other major ports were Yantian, Qingdao, Tianjin and Gungzhou. The total container cargo grew sharply even reaching almost 50 per cent growth rate in 1997 (Table 9.8). Table 9.9 shows the major characteristics of five container ports in China. It can be seen that Shanghai port has been most developed but the water depth is very shallow, limiting its potential future growth, whereas Yantian port is emerging as a new hub port, capitalising on the natural deep water which is available.

Approximately half of Chinese mainland exports are handled through Hong Kong and around 90 per cent of cargo emanating from South China passes through the port. However, two major ports at Shekou and Yantial are now in position to compete directly with Hong Kong. Yantian is operated by Hutchinson Whampoa and Shenzen Dongpen Industries as a joint venture. In terms of cost, exporting a 40 foot laden container originating in the Pearl River Delta direct from Shenzen to the USA saves US$175 compared to trans-shipment through Hong Kong, and for a 20 foot laden container to Europe, US$30 can be saved.[10]

Table 9.5: Ferry Services Between Korea and China, 2001

Route	Distance (miles)	Company	Ship Name	Capacity (people, TEU)	Frequency
Inchon/Weihai	238	Weidong	New Golden Bridge	656 (280)	3 times/ week
Inchon/Qingdao	330	Weidong	Xiang Xue Lan	392 (293)	2 times/ week
Inchon/Tianjin	460	Jinchon	Tian Ren	618 (247)	6 times/ month
Pusan/Yantai	540	Yantai	Zi Yu Lan	392 (293)	Once/ week
Kunsan/Yantai	273	Yantai	Zi Yu Lan	392 (293)	Once/ week
Inchon/Dalian	288	Dain	Dain	545 (170)	2 times/ week
Inchon/Dandong	284	Dandong	Oriental Pearl	405 (110)	2 times/ week
Inchon/Cheju/Shang hai	508	Shanghai-Inchon	Arafura Lily	290 (224)	Once/ week

Source: MOMAF.

It is noteworthy that Shanghai Port Authority has formed a new 50-50 equity joint venture (Shanghai Container Terminals Limited: henceforth SCT) with one of Hong Kong's largest companies, Hutchison Whampoa Limited and its subsidiary, Hong Kong International Terminals on August 12, 1993. SCT's total projected investment was 5.6 billion RMB with 2 billion RMB in registered capital and the joint venture term would last 50 years. The joint venture company took over operation of Shanghai's three main container terminal facilitates – Zhang Hua Bang, Jun Gong Lu, and Bao Shan – and its top priority was the conversion of five general cargo berths (two in Zhang Hua Bang and three in Jun Gong Lu) to container berths, thus totalling 12 berths on completion (Table 9.10). At the same time, the company looked into potential sites in the municipality for new container terminals, including Wai Gao Qiao in Pudong and Jin Shan Zai along Hangzhou Bay.

---

[10] Cullinane, K.P. (2000).

Table 9.6: Container Throughput by Port in Korea (TEU, %)

Year	National Total	Pusan	Inchon	Oolsan	Kwangyang	Others
1995	4,800,977 (100.0)	4,502,596 (93.8)	236.641 (4.9)	42.567	-	19,173 (0.4)
1996	5,202,898 (100.0)	4,760,507 (91.5)	348,727 (6.7)	47,003 (0.9)	-	46,661 (0.9)
1997	5,820,725 (100.0)	5,233,880 (89.9)	432,795 (7.4)	93,009 (1.6)	-	61,041 (1.1)
1998	6,371,535 (100.0)	5,752,955 (90.3)	401,536 (6.3)	125,829 (2.0)	32,135 (0.5)	59,080 (0.9)
1999	7,393,323 (100.0)	6,310,664 (85.4)	447,162 (6.0)	149,493 (2.0)	415,399 (5.6)	70,605 (1.0)

Brackets: portion of each port out of the national total.
Coastal container cargoes (domestic trade) excluded.
Source: Author.

Table 9.7: Characteristics of Specialised Container Terminals in Pusan and Kwangyang

	The Port of Pusan					Kwang-yang
	Jasung-dae	Shinsundae	Gamman	Uam	Kamchon	
Construction period	74-96	85-97	91-97	95-99	88-97	87-97
Start of Operation	Sept 1978	June 1991	April 1994	Sept 1996	Nov 1997	Jul 1998
Operator	HMM	PECT	4+ companies	WTC	HJ	4+ companies
Quay length	1,447 m	1,200 m	1,400 m	500 m	600 m	1,400 m
Water depth	12.5 m	14-15 m	15 m	11 m	13 m	15 m
Annual Capacity	1 million TEU	1.28 million TEU	1.2 million TEU	300 K TEU	370 K TEU	960 K TEU
Berthing Capacity	5,0000 dwt*4; 10,000 dwt*1	50,000dwt *4	50,000 dwt*4	20,000 dwt*1 5,000 dwt*2	50,000 dwt*2	50,000 dwt*4
Container Cranes	12	11	12	4	4	8

+ HJ (Hanjin), HMM (Hyundai Merchant Marine), Sebang, Daehan Tongwoon.
Source: Author.

Shanghai Port Authority has been developing Wai Gao Qiao (WGQ) as a new main container terminal since 1991, completing its first and second phase development plan. The WGQ terminal is scheduled to be expanded in two more phases until the year 2003, providing a capacity of 2.4 million TEU. In addition, the port authority has been considering a deep water port in Daxiao Yangsan area with a capacity of 22.4 million TEU by the year 2020. This area is at present composed of two small islands, therefore the new port has to be built requiring a great deal of land-filling and dredging so that the islands can be connected to be used as the quay structure. The port authority awaits the approval of city government (Table 9.11).

Table 9.8: Container Throughput in 10 Major Ports of China (000 TEU)

Port	1996	1997	1998	1999
Shanghai	1,923	2,530	3,066	4,200
Yantian	353	638	1,040	1,580
Qingdao	810	1,031	1,213	1,500
Tianjin	823	935	1,018	1,300
Guangzhou	547	687	848	1,177
Xiamen	400	546	654	840
Dalian	416	455	525	700
Shekou	90	214	463	601
Ningbou	202	257	353	600
Fuzhou	165	225	253	320
Total	7,400	10,774	13,158	17,710
Growth rate (%)	-	*45.64*	*22.09*	*34.59*

Sources: Hyoung-Geun Kim (2000), *Containerisation International Yearbook* (2000), *Cargo Systems* (2000).

Shanghai's weakest point used to be the shallow water so that a vessel of 2,000 TEU could call at the port only at high tide. The Ministry of Communications and the Shanghai Municipal Government ordered a technical study on the improvement of the fairway at the mouth of the Yanzi Jiang River and the deepening of the Hangzhou Bay fairway up to a water depth of 12.5 metres in order for the third and fourth-generation container vessels to pass.[11] Consequently it deepened the water depth from 10.5 metres to 12.5 metres in the Zhang Hua Bang Terminal and from 8.5 metres to 9.4 metres in the Bao Shan Terminal, respectively during the late 1990s. However, the water depth in the approach channel was only 7 metres deep so the port deepened the channel to 8.5 metres from July 1st, 2000. However, the water depth is still not deep enough to accommodate super post-Panamax vessels like those of the 5,000-6,000 TEU class, which require 15 metre water depth. Shanghai expects container growth of 1 million TEUs every year in the coming five years.

[11] Hu, L. (1993)

The container volumes in 1999 already surpassed capacity by one million TEU and this is to be further worsened in the future without a breakthrough development plan. To resolve this problem, the port authority has been considering a new site in the Daxiao Yangsan islands area for some years now but its implementation is still questionable and has been protracted so far.

Table 9.9: Major Characteristics of Five Container Ports in China

	Shanghai	Tianjin	Qingdao	Dalian	Yantian[+]
Terminals	3	1	1	2	2
Berths	NA	4	5	7	6
Quay Length (m)	2,281	1,300	1,189	918	1,900
Water Depth (m)	9.4-12.5	12	6-13	12-14	15-15.5
Ship/shore cranes (Ton x No)	35.5T x 1 35T x 5 30.5T x 3 30T x 6	40T x 2[a]	40.5T x 2 45.5T x 1	30.5T x 2 super post Panamax x 7	41T x 62
Yard Storage Capacity (TEU)	60,800	22,100	6,840	30,566 +[b]	25,000 +[c]

Source: *Containerisation International Yearbook* (2002).
+: Phase II container terminal was due to be completed by the end of 1999.
[a]: In addition to ship/shore container cranes, there are five mobile cranes (40t x 1; 25t x 4) and 13 yard cranes (40t x 7; 40.5t x 6).
[b]: No data were available about storage at Dayaowan Container Terminal.
[c]: 2nd phase data were not available.

In this respect, it is noteworthy that Yantian has enough water depth for these class vessels and is well equipped with a great number of container cranes. What is more, the Port of Yantian has on-dock railway track which links up with the Yantian and Pighu Nan Railway station which in turn connects to JingGuan railway at Pinghu Nan and Jingjiu railway at Chang-Ping.[12] In short, the Port of Yantian has all the major factors to be a hub port in terms of water depth, modernised cranes and an on-dock railway system for long-distance inland transportation; therefore, it appears to have great potential to take on a fully-fledged function in the Chinese container transport network in the near future. Although Dalian, Qingdao and Tianjin have relatively more advantageous water depths than Shanghai, due to their geographical location, ocean-going container vessels of foreign flags are less likely to directly call at them and as a consequence they are more likely to function as feeder service ports.

As for the China Land Bridge, the TCR was connected with the TSR in Novosibirsk in August, 1990, when a new line of 460 km was constructed

---

[12] *Containerisation International Yearbook*, 2000, 139.

from Urumqi to Alataw Shankou (border of China with Kazakhstan) and so it became possible for cargoes between Europe and Far Eastern Asia to pass through the Chinese railway and then to be connected with the TSR destined for Europe and/or Asia. The total length of the railway is 10,700 km inclusive of the TSR and China is responsible for 4,111 km encompassing six provinces including Jiangsu, Anhui, Henan, Shaanxi, Gansu and Xinjiang from Lianyungang/Shanghai through Xian, Lanzhou, Urumqi to Alataw Shankou.

Table 9.10: Shanghai Container Terminal Facilities

	Zhang Hua Bang	Jun Gong Lu	Bao Shan	Total
Quay Length (m)	783	858	640	**2,281**
Total Area (sq.m)	303,000	337,000	218,000	**858,000**
CFS Shed Area (sq.m)	6,841	6,841	10,426	**24,108**
Yard Capacity (TEU)	22,000	23,000	15,800	**60,800**
Gantry Cranes	5	6	4	**15**
Water Depth (m)	12.5	10.5	9.4	**9.4-12.5**

Source: *Containerisation International Yearbook* (2000).

Table 9.11: Terminal Developments in Shanghai Pudong and Daxiao

Terminal	Period	Quay length (m)	Gantry cranes	Water depth (m)	Total area (m²)	Capacity (TEU)
WGQ I	91-93	900	7	12.5	500,000	1,200
WGQ II	97-99	900	6	12.5	1,000,000	1,200
WGQ III	99-01	700	7	12.5	600,000	800
WGQ IV	00-03	1,250	12	13.0	1,000,000	1,600
DAXIAO	01-20	-	-	15.0	-	20,000
Total	-	**3,750**	**42**	-	**3,100,000**	**24,800**

Source: Author.

It is reported that the TCR can reduce the transportation distance from Pusan to Rotterdam by about 1,930 km compared with the TSR, with a resultant cut of about 20 per cent in transportation cost.[13] China and Korea agreed to co-operate in using the TCR and the two countries have explored the possibilities of transporting cargoes between Europe and Far Eastern Asia through the TCR. However, the performance using the TCR has proved difficult mainly because of China's problems in reaching agreement on transit costs with Kazakhstan and also the lack of trans-shipment facilities in Alataw

---

[13] Hong, S. (1992)

Shankou and Druzhba stations (the latter is on the border of Kazakhstan and China). The Druzhba transhipment station, opened in 1990 already exceeded its capacity, sending about 1.2 million tons of goods to China and receiving about 300,000 tons of finished goods from China. The cargoes destined for Europe can be transported using the TCR in three ways, namely, Trans-Rail (rail and rail), Trans-Sea (rail and sea) and Tracon (rail and truck).

Meanwhile, a survey was conducted of the 600 biggest Korean companies trading with China in August, 1993 asking them for their views on the major inconveniences of the trade.[14] Most complaints resulted from customs clearance, inland transportation, sea transportation, stevedoring and stuffing and stripping in the order of magnitude of the complaints. One illustration is that for customs clearance, very long lists of documents were required and processing of documentation was also deemed to be too slow.

Conclusion

During the last decade, the economic dynamism of the Yellow Sea Rimland countries has been a focus of world attention. The recent free movement of capital, technology, commodities and labour are facilitating the formation of the Yellow Sea Economic Bloc.[15] For this reason, the Yellow Sea rimlands are now viewed as forming a well defined economic corridor in the Asia-Pacific region in the eyes of the human geographer.

Concerns in the region have been expressed about the adequacy of the infrastructure and efficiency in meeting society's needs at the lowest total costs in terms of the country's resources. If infrastructure investments are to be optimised and if they are to respond to the greater complexity of economies, more intense international competition and their failure to meet user needs, individual countries must re-examine the framework through which port services are delivered.[16]

This paper has reviewed how maritime co-operation between Korea and China has progressed thus far and what the contemporary issues are. Since the 'open door policy' of the Chinese government has been adopted, international trade between China and other countries seems to have exploded as is typified by that between Korea and China showing 43 per cent annual growth rate between 1979 and 1999. Ten years after the introduction of the open door policy, the maiden voyage was on the Yellow Sea carrying the first seaborne

[14] Internal survey data by KOTRA conducted during August 1993 of the 600 biggest Korean companies in volume trading with China.
[15] Hong, *op. cit.*
[16] Rimmer, *Ibid.*

cargoes, which accelerated the ensuing maritime trade, resulting in currently 28 container vessels and seven ferries in operation. Therefore, container cargoes increased from 56,252 TEU in 1990 to 925,751 TEU in 1999 at an annual growth rate of 36.5 per cent between the two countries. To accommodate bigger vessels and sharply increasing cargoes and/or implicitly to be a regional hub, the two countries have developed and expanded their port facilities remarkably. Likewise, the inland container transport network has also been expanded, particularly by the trans-continental railway systems such as the TCR and TSR. Noticeably, South and North Korea have recently explored reconnecting the former railway to connect the TKR and TCR. All these developments from ports to the inland network will eventually make the regional transport network more efficient and in turn will intensify regional co-operation.

Accordingly, maritime co-operation between Korea and China will play a key role in contributing to strengthening regional co-operation in East Asia. Undoubtedly, the co-operation will benefit not only the two countries, but also neighbouring ones and ultimately the whole global society. In conclusion, co-operation should be further expedited in the foreseeable future. One practical way of further maritime co-operation between the two countries is to use Korean container ports as the major trans-shipment ports for Chinese cargoes. China's container transport has shown almost 40 per cent growth and this trend is expected to continue for many decades. Compared with this cargo growth, container port development is not enough to handle these enormous cargoes. In this respect, Korea is willing to develop several terminals to be used as the trans-shipment port for these Chinese cargoes. Recent years have witnessed major container trans-shipment cargoes, particularly from North China using Korean ports due to their vicinity and lower port rates as well as an efficient transport network with major shipping trunk routes around the world. Therefore, both countries are likely to further benefit from increased trans-shipment cargo co-operation.

References

Cargo Systems (2000) July.
Containerisation International Yearbooks, 1996-2002.
Cullinane, K.P. (2000) The Competitive Position of the Port of Hong Kong, *Proceedings of KASS and KOMARES International Symposium: Challenge of the World Shipping and Response of the Korean Shipping in the 21st Century*, November 10-11, Seoul, Korea.

De, W.D. (1993) Asia-Pacific Economy and Development and Potential of Tianjin Port, *Asia-Pacific Ports Symposium Proceeding,* Kobe, 255-263.

Dong, W.D. (1993) Dalian Port: Present and Future, *Asia-Pacific Ports Symposium Proceeding,* Kobe, 203-211.

Hacheong, Y. (1991) *Proceedings of KIEP* conference.

Hong, S. (1992) Ocean Industry Co-operation in the Yellow Sea: Strategy and Implications, *Ocean Policy Research,* 7, 2, 277-305.

Hu, L.H. (1993) Shanghai Port Greeting the 21st Century, *Asia-Pacific Ports Symposium Proceeding,* Kobe, 239-247.

Jeon, K. (1993) Development Strategy of the Port of Pusan Including Competitive Port Management and Other Recent Issues of the port, in *Asia-Pacific Ports Symposium Proceeding,* Kobe, 523-532.

Jon, J. (1992) Regional Economic Development and the Role of Maritime Transportation, *Proceedings of the SLOC Study Group – Korea.*

KIET (1991) *The Possibility of North-east Asian Economic Co-operation.*

Korea Herald (2002) February 20th.

Kim, H-G. (2000) *Weekly Maritime Information,* Korea Maritime Institute, November 20th.

Nam, S. (2000) *Competition and Complementarity in Northeast Asian Trade: Korea's Perspective,* Working Paper 200-02, KIEP.

Noland, M. (1991) The Northeast Asian Economy in the 1990s: Economic Outlook and Development Potential, *Proceedings of KIEP conference.*

Rimmer, P.J. (1993) Restructuring Port Operations in the Asia-Pacific Region, *IAPH publications,* 1-19.

Rimmer, P.J. (1993) *Taiwan's Future as a Regional Transport Hub,* monograph.

Yang, J. and Kim, H. (2000) *Issues in Korean Trade 1999: Trends, Disputes and Trade Policy,* Working Paper 200-01, KIEP.

10 International Market Entry Strategies in China: Lessons from Ocean Shipping and Logistics Multinationals

Photis M. Panayides
Hong Kong Polytechnic University, Hong Kong

Introduction

The ocean liner shipping industry is characterised by global competition on a number of dimensions including price, marketing and strategic aspects. Competition has become fierce with more companies entering the ocean shipping business and vying for the same customers and in the same markets. As a result companies have sought to expand their line of activities through vertical integration in the supply chain by engaging in inland transportation and logistics. The global nature of the industry, the strategies of expansion and diversification and intense competition are closely associated with the quest and motivation of multinational shipping and logistics corporations to enter new markets. Despite the propensity for foreign direct investment (FDI) and international market entry and the importance of the underlying motives and strategies for multinational shipping corporations, there has been little attention paid to the issues from a scientific perspective.

The aim of this chapter is to explore the determinants and market entry strategies of ocean shipping and logistics corporations in China. China has been chosen for this analysis because it is a large emerging market of critical importance to ocean shipping and logistics multinationals. In addition, the sheer size of the market and recent entry to the World Trade Organisation (WTO) suggest that trade, and hence, transport and logistics, will play an important role in China's economic development.

This chapter begins with an analysis of Foreign Direct Investment (FDI) in China and its significance for the development of the country's transport and logistics infrastructure. The arguments underpin the importance of market entry and FDI by shipping and logistics multinationals. The theoretical literature on FDI is reviewed and a theoretical framework is revealed and empirically examined in the context of shipping and logistics multinationals. A case study method is adopted and the results provide practical, policy-making and research implications.

The Importance of FDI and Transport and Logistics Development in China

A number of scholars have long recognised and argued that FDI is one of the main forces driving economic growth (Blomstrom *et al.*, 1992; De Gregorio, 1992). FDI is of particular importance to developing countries (Balasubramanyan *et al.*, 1996) and to China specifically (Chen *et al.*, 1995; Luo, 1998; Wu, 2000).

The Importance of FDI

According to the Organisation for Economic Co-operation and Development (OECD), FDI has been a defining feature of the world economy over the past two decades. FDI has grown at an unprecedented rate inducing greater competition among host economies. As a result, global flows reached a historic high of US$340 billion in 1996 (OECD, 1998). The importance of FDI for host economies is reflected in the scientifically determined assertion that FDI is more efficient in contributing to economic growth of the host country than domestic investment. De Gregorio (1992) shows, in panel data of 12 Latin American countries, that FDI is about three times more efficient than domestic investment. Blomstrom *et al.* (1992) also found a strong effect of FDI on economic growth in less developed countries. Findlay (1978) postulates that FDI increases the rate of technical progress in the host country through a 'contagion' effect from the more advanced technology, management practices etc., used by the foreign firms. Wang (1990) incorporates this idea into a model more in line with the neo-classical growth framework, by assuming that the increase in knowledge applied to production is determined as a function of FDI. Borensztein *et al.* (1998) found that FDI is an important vehicle for the transfer of technology, contributing to growth in larger measure than domestic investment.

FDI in China

Since 1979 a continuing inflow of FDI has played a pivotal role in China's economic growth. Luo and Tan (1997) note that during the period 1979-1995, Chinese authorities approved the establishment of some 258,444 FDI projects involving US$393.04 billion in foreign capital. About 120,000 foreign-funded enterprises representing US$133.04 billion have commenced operations (Foreign Investment in China, 1996). Probably the most remarkable effort yet to attract FDI occurred in October 1986 with the promulgation by the State Council of the 'Provision to Encourage Foreign Direct Investment' ('the 22 Articles'). The provision offered a series of preferential policies and encouraged the development of the Economic and Technological Development Zones (ETDZ) in every region. A detailed review of the history of China's economic development in relation to FDI and associated policies can be found in Chen *et al.* (1995) and Luo (1998).

The unquestionable positive contribution of FDI in the economy of China has been empirically analysed by a number of scholars. Chen *et al.* (1995), for instance, have determined empirically the benefits of FDI to the Chinese economy. They posit that the cumulative total of US$34 billion of actual FDI that occurred by 1992, contributed to economic growth by augmenting the resources available for capital formation, by contributing to export earnings, by forcing domestic manufacturers to compete globally and by progressively inducing plant managers and government officials to adopt the rules of a market economy. They also cite the diffusion of management and marketing skills, the adoption of legislation promoting market economics and the substantial transfer of low and intermediate technologies as direct benefits of FDI in China. Dees (1998) found that FDI affects China's growth through the diffusion of ideas.

Transportation and Logistics in China

The importance of transport modes and logistics systems development in China is underpinned by the fact that transportation infrastructure and logistics-related systems and superstructures facilitate trade. With the advent of China to WTO status and the market-oriented reforms that seem to be an on-going process, albeit at a relatively gradual pace, the need for systems to facilitate trade seems to be self-evident. Facilitation and the consequent increase in trade will also have a significant positive impact on attracting inward FDI. In fact causal links have been empirically identified between the growth in China's imports and inward FDI from a home country/region, which in turn causes the growth of exports from China (Liu *et al.*, 2001; Zhang and Felmingham, 2001).

Despite the remarkable economic growth of China, particularly since 1978, the development of the country's transport infrastructure has fallen seriously behind. The demand for transport of people and goods has exceeded the capacity of its road and railway systems. At around 0.04km per person, highway density in China is less than in India (0.05km) and significantly less than Japan, the UK and the US. The port and shipping infrastructure is also underdeveloped in China. Of the country's 60 major coastal ports, only 446 of a total of 1,322 berths are deepwater (China Statistics, 2000). In addition, the increase in trading activity led to a dramatic expansion of containerisation since the early 1990s. In particular, containerised shipments rose from 1.56 million TEUs (twenty foot equivalent unit container) to 10 million TEUs in 1997. Container shipping will act as a catalyst for the development of logistics in China. Figure 10.1 illustrates the close relationship between economic development and the increase in trade and transport (containerisation), in China.

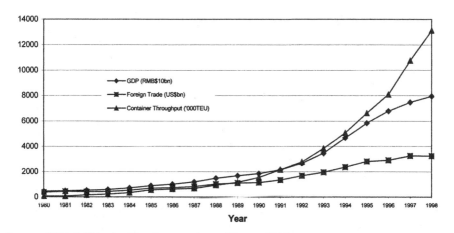

Source: *China's Shipping Development Annual Report 1998*

Figure 10.1: Trends in Economic Growth, Trade and Container Throughput in China

FDI as a Catalyst for Transport Development in China

Although China has plans to improve its transport infrastructure, the World Bank estimates that it will not be able to meet its transport requirements until at least the year 2020 (Business Asia, 1994). Zhan (1993) emphasises the importance of a well-functioning physical infrastructure, including transportation, telecommunications and public utilities for improving the attractiveness to FDI, whilst recognising that the state of these facilities in China presents a serious impediment to FDI. In fact, it is strenuously suggested that the recent priority given by the Government towards the development of infrastructure should be supported through the provision of incentives for FDI in infrastructure development. Ta, Choo and Sum (2000) state:

> ...while China presents a huge market potential and an attractive 'low cost environment' for foreign firms and investors, it may still be unprofitable if there are serious problems in getting the products to the customers on time and in good condition. An underdeveloped transport infrastructure, therefore, can pose a serious obstacle to a large country like China that is in transition to a market economy and requires foreign investments.

Speece and Kawahara (1995) express similar sentiments on the problem of transportation infrastructure in China. The fact that transport, shipping and logistics in China are major determinants for economic growth and in need of capital investment is evident and undisputed. FDI by multinational shipping corporations will have direct economic benefits and long-term significance in terms of improvement of infrastructure, systems and organisational techniques in the shipping and logistics sector. It will also increase the attractiveness of the country for FDI in other sectors. Zhan (1993) states:

> A well-functioning physical infrastructure, including transportation...can greatly increase a host country's attractiveness to FDI.

It follows that the establishment of policies for attracting FDI by multinational shipping and logistics corporations is imperative. Bearing in mind the propensity of shipping conglomerates to invest in China, it seems of high practical importance to assess the determinants of FDI in China's shipping and logistics as a means for determining optimal policies.

Foreign Direct Investment: A Review of the Learned Literature

Theoretical Approaches for Evaluating FDI

A range of theoretical perspectives has been utilised to explain the level and pattern of FDI or multinational enterprise (MNE) activity. These theoretical perspectives range from the mainstream economic theories (Hymer, 1960; 1976; Kindleberger, 1969; Vernon, 1966; Caves, 1971), and internalisation models (Buckley and Casson, 1976; 1985; Rugman, 1981) to the eclectic paradigm (Dunning, 1988a; 1988b; 1993). General taxonomies on the extant theoretical literature are documented in Buckley and Casson (1985), Cantwell (1991), Dunning (1993; 1997; 2000) and Grosse and Behrman (1992).

Motives for FDI may be summarised in a taxonomy devised by Behrman (1972). The taxonomy identifies four types of MNE activity viz. the resource seekers, the market seekers, efficiency seekers and strategic asset or capability seekers. The resource seekers are motivated by their need for cheaper resources including physical, human, technological or organisational resources. The second group comprises those companies that seek to protect or exploit new markets, motivated by prospects for growth and large market share, to establish presence in a new market prior to competitors or to counteract similar action by competitors. Multinational shipping and logistics corporations may primarily fall into this second category. The intention of the efficiency seekers on the other hand is to take advantage of different factor endowments, economic systems, policies and market structures to concentrate production in a limited number of locations. The strategic asset seekers may engage in FDI as a means for sustaining or enhancing their international competitiveness.

Hymer (1960; 1976), who challenged the model of perfect competition and concentrated on a firm's ability to hinder competition in a market, postulated the first fully coherent theory of FDI. On this basis, Kindleberger (1969) developed the 'market imperfections model', which states that for FDI to thrive the foreign company must possess specific advantages outweighing the disadvantages of being foreign and that the market for those advantages must be imperfect. Such advantages include knowledge, economies of scale and product differentiation. Internalisation theory is based on transaction cost economics (Williamson 1975; 1985) and is concerned with explaining why cross border transactions are organised by hierarchies (FDI) rather than by market forces. According to the internalisation model, the reason for multinational enterprises (hereafter MNEs) engaging in FDI arises from market failures stemming from the existence of transaction costs that make direct investment in subsidiaries more feasible than market contracting (Buckley, 1988). The internalisation paradigm suggests that MNE is the efficient alternative to the lack of free trade (arising from market imperfections).

The market versus hierarchy organisation of production (internalisation) was further expanded by the eclectic paradigm of Dunning (1980; 1988a; 1988b) who attempted to analyse the pattern and determinants of FDI in terms of ownership, location and internalisation (OLI). Ownership advantages are those that are specific to a particular firm and that enable it to take advantage of investment opportunities abroad. Location advantages are those advantages specific to a country, which dictate the choice of production site. Internalisation advantages determine the market versus hierarchy (FDI) organisation of production as explained above. In fact, the OLI approach seems to encompass all the major issues relating to FDI as evidenced by the variables examined in most of the empirical studies undertaken.

Empirical Surveys on MNE Activity and FDI Determinants

The main themes of empirical examinations in FDI include the motives and modes of market entry, ownership, location and internalisation as well as other specific determinants that may be applicable to particular host countries, industrial sectors and situations.

Market entry mode A number of studies have sought to associate the chosen mode of market entry with the OLI framework (Agarwal and Ramaswani, 1992; Caves, 1982; Davidson and McFetridge, 1985; Kimura, 1989; Kogut and Singh, 1988; Terpstra and Yu, 1988).

Studies of mode of foreign entry examine a broad range of possibilities. Different levels of control are considered ranging from greenfield investments, wholly owned subsidiaries (WOSs) through joint ventures to non-equity alliances (Agarwal and Ramaswami, 1992; Anderson and Gatignon, 1986; Hennart and Park, 1993; Hennart and Reddy, 1997; Larimo, 1995). A number of factors have been theorised (Anderson and Gatignon, 1986) and shown to affect the mode of entry decision (Kogut and Singh, 1988; Li and Guisinger, 1991; Mudambi, 1995; Woodstock *et al.*, 1994).

Various factors may account for the choice of a particular mode for entering a foreign market. For instance, according to some authors, the choice may depend on product characteristics such as degree of differentiation, importance, age, and technological content (Davidson,

1982; Gatignon and Anderson, 1987; Goodnow, 1985; Stopford and Wells, 1972). Certain firm characteristics such as size and resources, degree of diversification and corporate policies may also have an impact (Davidson, 1982; Root, 1987; Stopford and Wells, 1972). Finally, entry mode choice by firms may also be determined by external environmental factors: host country trade and investment restrictions, host country market size, host country geographic and cultural distance and exchange rate fluctuations (Aliber, 1970; Baek and Kwok, 2002; Bauershmidt, *et al*. 1985; Goodnow and Hansz, 1972; Stopford and Wells, 1972). In addition a number of behavioural determinants have been postulated to affect international marketing decisions, involvement in foreign markets, choice of markets and choice of foreign market entry modes (Aharoni, 1966; Cavusgil, 1980; Erramilli and Rao, 1990; Johanson and Vahlne, 1977). In addition the initial mode of entry may not be related to subsequent sequential entries (Chang and Rosenzweig, 2001). Two major theoretical perspectives have emerged as viable frameworks for examining MNEs' entry mode choice (Gomes-Casseres, 1990; Tallman and Shenkar, 1994). The first framework is transaction-cost analysis (TCA) and has been used in several empirical studies of Western MNE's entry mode choice (e.g. Davidson and McFeteridge, 1985; Anderson and Gatignon, 1986; Anderson and Coughlin, 1987; Erramilli, 1991; Erramilli and Rao, 1993). The second framework is bargaining power (BP) theory which views entry mode choice as an outcome of negotiations between the firm and the government of the host country. This framework has undergone some empirical testing in the entry mode choice context (e.g. Lecraw, 1984; Gomes-Casseres, 1990).

Location In terms of location, studies have addressed the issue of choice between countries and choice of location within countries. The attractiveness of a market has been characterised in terms of its market potential and investment risk as well as resource abundance in the geographical location. Zhao and Zhu (1998) found that foreign business agglomeration creates a gravitational effect to draw new foreign investors in the region and denotes low uncertainty and risk of doing business in that area. Wu and Strange (2000) found that the location of foreign insurance companies in China is influenced by proximity to the regulatory authority, openness in the award of operating licenses, current and future market demand, and the presence of other foreign investment. Cheng and Kwan (2000) found that Special Economic Zones and other such key areas in China have a positive effect on FDI. In addition, the potential for technology spillovers to local competitors may contribute to a decision by strong foreign investors to locate further away (Chung, 2001).

Internalisation Ownership advantages are the superior assets and skills of firms that can earn economic rents high enough to counter the higher cost of servicing foreign markets. Ownership advantages include firm size, multinational experience and the firm's ability to develop differentiated products. A firm possessing such assets is likely to choose higher control modes for market entry (Anderson and Coughlan, 1987; Caves, 1982; Coughlan, 1985). The internalisation paradigm suggests that the multinational enterprise is the efficient alternative to the lack of free trade (Rugman, 1980). Under the internalisation paradigm, firm specific endowments or advantages internal to the MNE together with industry specific factors lead to FDI. If those advantages were not to be realised then FDI may have not been an attractive proposition for multinationals.

In high market potential countries, investment modes are expected to provide greater long-term profitability to a firm, compared to non-investment modes. This may be achieved through the opportunity to achieve economies of scale and consequently lower marginal cost of production (Sabi, 1988). Investment risk reflects the uncertainty over the economic and political conditions prevailing in the host country. Government policies are critical to the survival and profitability of a company in a host country. If government policies impede FDI, companies are more likely to pursue entry via non-investment options. The issue of internalisation, which concerns the retention of assets and skills within the firm and the problems associated with transaction costs, plays a role in choosing between low and high control modes of market entry. Low control modes may be considered superior since they allow a firm to benefit from scale economies whilst avoiding the problems of integration. However, they may be associated with higher costs due to bounded rationality, external uncertainty and contractual risks (Anderson and Weitz, 1986). Under these conditions, sole venture modes provide better control due to retention of the assets and skills within the firm.

Other determinants Various other studies sought to identify additional and more specific determinants of FDI as they would apply to certain industries or host countries. Oxelheim *et al.* (2001) for instance, argue that the FDI literature and the OLI paradigm in particular would be enriched if finance-specific factors are explicitly incorporated as drivers of FDI. In the case of developing countries, the size of the market and lower wage costs seem to be significant determinants of FDI flows (Schneider and Frey, 1985;

Wheeler and Mody, 1992). Mixed results have been found with respect to the effect of socio-political variables such as political risk and instability (see Aharoni, 1966; Levis, 1979; Lucas, 1993; Wheeler and Mody, 1992). Business operating conditions, which may be shaped by government policy, and export orientation have also been found to influence FDI flows (Brewer, 1993; Hein, 1992). Tatoglu and Glaister (1998) determine empirically the motivation for foreign equity ventures in Turkey in relation to ownership pattern, market entry mode, country of origin and sector and size of the investment. They found 13 determinants grouped into four factors, viz. transaction-costs, production efficiency, market development and quality control and financially viability. Dees (1998) found that domestic market size, cost advantages and openness to the rest of the world influence inward FDI. Cheng and Kwan (2000) test five sets of variables for determining the location of FDI in China. These include: (a) access to national and regional markets; (b) wage costs (quality of workers, labour productivity, labour market conditions, unemployment, unionisation); (c) policy towards FDI (taxes, Special Economic Zones); (d) availability and quality of infrastructure (roads, railways, ports); (e) economies of agglomeration. They found that the size of a region's market has a positive effect but wage cost has a negative effect on FDI. Good infrastructure attracts FDI and education has a positive effect albeit not significant statistically. Special Economic Zones and other such key areas also have a positive effect on FDI.

The Case of Multinational Ocean Shipping and Logistics Corporations

According to *The Foreign Companies in China Yearbook 2000/01*, there are 52 foreign companies in China grouped under the industry classification 'transport'. Companies unrelated to freight transport are excluded. These companies are those WOSs and joint ventures set up in China (excluding Hong Kong and Taiwan) by multinational shipping corporations. Table 10.1 shows the country of origin of these companies.

The 52 companies originate from a total of 16 foreign countries. The largest group of companies comes from the United States, which accounts for 10 firms and 19.23 per cent of the total number of companies. The second largest group comes from Germany, which accounts for seven firms and 13.46 per cent of all companies, followed by the United Kingdom and Switzerland. Each country accounts for six firms and a total of 11.54 per cent of all companies. The companies of the three largest groups (United

States, Germany, United Kingdom and Switzerland) represent over half (55.77 per cent) of the total number of companies.

Table 10.1: Country of Origin of Multinational Shipping Corporations in China

Home country	No. of companies per country	% of total no. of companies
USA	10	19.23
Germany	7	13.46
Switzerland, UK	6	11.54
Sweden, France	3	5.77
Hong Kong, Denmark, Norway, Germany + Hong Kong	2	3.85
Austria, Australia, South Korea, Iran, Japan, Netherlands, Poland + China, Denmark + China, UK + Netherlands	1	1.92
Total no. of companies	52	100

Table 10.2 illustrates the location of the offices of these companies in China. The 52 foreign companies have established a total of 198 offices in China. Shanghai is the most popular city with 42 offices accounting for 21.21 per cent of the total number of offices. Beijing is the second most popular with 26 offices, which accounts for 13.13 per cent of the total number of offices. The third popular cities are Dalian and Shenzhen as each has 14 offices and represents 7.07 per cent of the total number of offices followed by Guangzhou with 12 offices (6.06 per cent). The top five cities (Shanghai, Beijing, Dalian, Shenzhen and Guangzhou) represent over half (54.55 per cent) of the total number of offices.

Table 10.3 illustrates the representation in China of a sample of foreign ocean shipping and logistics multinationals. In terms of encouraging FDI by shipping and logistics companies, the official position has been that ports and transportation projects are open to FDI, including investment and participation in the management of joint ventures and setting up WOSs. In fact a point is made of having all major international shipping companies represented in the most important harbours of China including Shanghai, Tianjin, Guangzhou, Dalian and Qingdao. Despite this it has been recognised that:

> although foreign companies are officially permitted to handle transport operations, in practice, a lot of resistance comes from governmental bureaucrats (Luo, 1998).

Table 10.2: Location of Multinational Shipping Companies'
Offices in China

Location	Number of offices per city	Total number of offices (%)
Shanghai	42	21.21
Beijing	26	13.13
Dalian	14	7.07
Shenzhen	14	7.07
Guangzhou	12	6.06
Nanjing, Tianjin	9	9.10
Fuzhou, Ningbo, Xiamen	6	9.09
Qingdao	5	2.53
Wuhan	4	2.02
Chengdu, Nantong, Shantou, Zhangjiagang, Chongqing, Hangzhou	3	9.12
Quingdao, Lianyungang, Shenyang, Nanning, Shunde, Zhuhai, Zhongshan	2	7.07
Dongguan, Jiangmen, Rongqi, Fangchenggang, Harbin, Kunming, Wenzhou, Hefei, Xian, Yangzhou, Zhengzhou, Quanzhou, Hainan	1	6.63
Total no. of offices	198	100

The objectives of China for attracting FDI, increasing trade and developing the sea and land transport and logistics infrastructure, render an analysis of the potential for investment by multinational shipping and logistics corporations of significant value.

The Research Objectives

The prospects presented by the sheer size and current state of developments in China's markets, together with the requirement for investment in transport and logistics infrastructure, suggest the need and potential interest in FDI by multinational shipping and logistics corporations. The major questions posed in considering FDI in China are related to the benefits and objectives sought by potential investors, the method of market entry that includes issues of ownership and internalisation, and the location and potential hindrances that may be presented by current legislation and policy. The review of the FDI literature validates these questions from a theoretical perspective in that they have been considered in the multitude of previous studies on FDI. On the basis of the above, this study aims to explore the following issues in the context of multinational shipping and logistics corporations:

- The motives for entering and investing in China;
- The preferred location of establishment and the underlying reasons;
- The preferred modes of market entry including issues of ownership; and
- The possible hindrances to FDI in China's shipping and logistics markets.

Table 10.3: Selected Multinational Shipping Companies' Representation in China

Company	Branch offices	Headquarters	Market entry	WOS Status
APL	10	Beijing	1979	Yes
CMA CGM	7	Shanghai	1992	No
Maersk-Sealand	11	Beijing	1979	Yes
MOL	2	Shanghai	1995	No
PONL	7	Shanghai	1979	Yes

Source: *Containerisation International.*

Methodology

Empirical Approaches to the Study of FDI

Empirical studies of FDI are based on three approaches, viz. (a) micro-oriented econometric studies; (b) survey data analyses; and (c) aggregate econometric analyses. Each approach has its limitations and advantages. The determinant issues for deciding upon the most applicable approach are the research objectives and the context of the research study. An econometric approach may not be applicable in the context of the research objectives of this study. This is because the aim is to examine an industrial sector and not undertake an aggregate assessment of the determinants of FDI in general. In addition, there is the exploratory nature of the investigation and the need to identify factors rather than specify them *a priori* and test for their existence. Examination of the framework suggested above may include socio-political, regulatory and legislative variables and business-operating conditions that cannot be accurately assessed using an econometric model. Jun and Singh (1996) advocate the importance of qualitative studies for such assessments. Tatoglu and Glaister (1998) note that the literature gives little indication *a priori* of what to expect in terms of relative importance of a set of motivating factors for FDI activity. It follows that the factors as well as their importance need to be identified directly from the informants and this is particularly true for specific industrial sectors where research is carried out for the first time. Boddewyn *et al.* (1986) argue that particular attention must be paid to the application of FDI theories for international service firms due to the idiosyncratic characteristics of such industries. It follows that a field study would be most applicable in the context of this research. Dunning (1993) notes the role played by field studies in advancing the understanding of the determinants of FDI. In particular, he makes the case for the suitability of such an approach in cases where previous research in the area has been limited. He further notes that determinants for FDI identified by business respondents in field studies have been later incorporated into econometric models, whereas another contribution of these studies has been their ability to identify and evaluate less quantitative explanatory variables.

The Case Study Approach

Having considered the different available methods for conducting the empirical part of the research, the case study approach seems to offer most advantages in terms of achieving the research objectives. The case study method has been preferred because of:

- The limited number of multinational corporations that have actually made an entry into China's shipping and logistics industries. This means that obtaining in-depth data may be more useful than attempting to generalise on a wider population from a small sample.
- The limited current understanding and existing knowledge of the specific sector. More benefits would confer from a qualitative approach that will seek to explore issues that may later be the subject of justification-oriented research hypotheses.

The research objectives were addressed through the collection of primary and secondary data. The aim of the research method was to facilitate examination of the focal issues relating to FDI flows and the OLI framework in a shipping and logistics context through the study of a few cases. Primary data were collected through an investigation that included personal and telephone interviews with people at the upper echelon of the management hierarchy in eight multinational ocean shipping and logistics corporations. The ideal number of cases to study in research of this nature depends on the research objectives and may vary from a single case-study examining a number of issues in depth, to multiple cases examining one focal issue (Voss *et al.*, 2002). Eisenhardt (1995) suggests a sample of between four and 10 cases, a range supported by Remenyi *et al.* (1998). Since the aim is to explore issues in the specific industrial context and where possible replicate or contrast previous theoretical assertions, the cases were selected in accordance to replication logic rather than sampling logic (Eisenhardt, 1989; Yin, 1994). Hence, each case was selected so that it either:

- predicts similar results (a literal replication); or
- produces contrary results but for predictable reasons (a theoretical replication).

Imperative in the research was improvement of data quality and assessment of validity and reliability. For this purpose, the propositions by Leonard-Barton (1990) and Yin (1994) were adhered to. The propositions include observing whether predictions made about relationships are confirmed, using multiple sources of evidence, seeking triangulation and ensuring that the results obtained are reliable and will be obtained again if the study's operations are repeated.

The questions posed related to the OLI framework but were of an open-ended nature to encourage discussion. The interviews were not structured but in order to ensure that the same themes were covered for each firm, a protocol was employed. The latter improves data reliability (Voss *et al.*, 2002). The interviewees were encouraged to speak about their own company's experience primarily. During the interviews it became apparent that they were also willing to offer views about the general perceptions of people in the shipping and logistics industry and their experiences.

In analysing the data, the first step was to identify and summarise the beliefs and statements made by the respondents on the issues being tested on a case-by-case basis. Following this, the cases were compared in order to reveal patterns, similarities and differences. Cross-case analysis also increases the internal validity of the findings as the deliberate seeking of confirmation from multiple data sources leads to more reliable results. As a means of replication and further refinement a summary of the preliminary results was sent to the respondents who were asked to make additional comments. This together with the use of multiple cases augments construct and external validity and helps to guard against researcher bias.

Table 10.4: Characteristics of Participating Companies

	Company description	Services	Head-quarters	Size – Employees
1	Global transport, ocean ship	Integrated transportation, logistics,supply chain management (SCM),warehousing, cargo consolidation, freight forwarding.	Hong Kong	1,000
2	Global and regional transport/Hong Kong and China	Transport and Logistics, shop operation, SCM, chartering,sea/land/air freight forwarding.	Hong Kong	700
3	Logistics Hong Kong/China	Third –party Logistics	China	800
4	Global ocean shipping, transport	Ocean shipping, logistics, intermodal services	South Korea	
5	Global logistics	SCM, land/sea/air operations, cargo consolidation, IT and inventory services	USA (Shanghai-Asia)	680
6	Regional transport, ship-owners Hong Kong/China	Ship operation, feeder services, oil terminal operations	Hong Kong	400
7	Global transport, ocean shipping	Ocean transport, logistics, SCM, land/sea/air transport, insurance, agency	Japan (Shanghai-Asia)	750
8	Global, mail, express, logistics	SCM, warehousing, Transportation	Europe (Shanghai-Asia)	>10,000

Source: Author.

Results and Analysis of the Case Studies

Organisational Characteristics of the Companies

All eight companies selected for participation in the study provide transport and logistics services (amongst others) and have an established presence in China, albeit in various forms. Table 10.4 illustrates the main characteristics of the companies participating in the study. The data was collected during the interviews, as well as from secondary sources of information such as annual reports, brochures and the business press.

Motives

The main motive for entering the Chinese market as elicited by the interviewees, included the sheer size of the market and the business opportunities for growth and profitability that it presents, particularly in the logistics industry. The companies deemed the potential for logistics development to be presenting tremendous opportunities, which have been the catalyst for implementing the direct investment decision. It was also acknowledged, however, that barring the main population concentrations in cities like Shanghai and Beijing and the main port cities, logistics demand in China is still at an infant stage.

The large market and geographical distance between population centres present significant potential for logistics companies. The volume of imports and exports is very large and expands continuously. The huge population creates demand for various types of goods that need the means for quick transportation from production points to consumption centres. The size of the market seems to be the most important determinant for investment. Corroborating evidence for this assertion is provided by the studies of Grub *et al.* (1990), Zang (1995) and Dees (1998). The demand for logistics and transportation in China arises from the significant investment of foreign retail conglomerates in China. Foreign investment in the retail and manufacturing sectors induces a demand for investment in the logistics sector.

Interestingly, according to the interviewees, the lower cost of labour and the cheaper land-related costs in China are not significant determinants for logistics companies when compared to other industries. It was held that these factors are indirect determinants for investment in logistics, the latter being a derived demand from the need to transport manufactured goods and raw materials. This finding is rather contrary to past studies advocating that lower cost of labour is a significant determinant for FDI (Cushman, 1987).

However, Chen (1996) found that location choice in the Chinese context does not seem to have been influenced by consideration of labour cost differences or differences in allocative efficiency.

Another factor that seems to have played a significant role for the companies' decision to enter China was the recognition that important competitors were also eyeing up the market and about to enter or have already established their presence in the country. It follows that the motives of ocean shipping and logistics multinationals for investment in China, may include market seeking and to counteract competitors' strategies and/or position themselves for future strategic growth.

Location

FDI in particular sectors of the economy, may be encouraged by specific policies promulgated by the government. The Chinese policy is mainly characterised by the division of the country into three different economic zones. They include, Special Economic Zones (SEZs), Open Cities and other areas not grouped under SEZs or Open Cities. Many foreign investors are attracted by special privileges such as a favourable tax rate and greater infrastructure support available in the first two zones.

The emergent reasons for locating in a particular area or city include the presence of good infrastructure in terms of transport and communication networks as well as good port facilities that can offer opportunities for developing sea networks with other regions and countries. The companies mainly invested in the coastal areas of China and in cities such as Guangzhou, Shanghai, Tianjin, Dalian and Qingdao. Compared with other parts of China, these cities have better infrastructure that supports transportation of cargoes. They also have good ports with sufficient terminal facilities able to cater for the large and increasing volume of exports. For non-coastal cities the critical factors are the existence of a developed or developing commercial business centre and the presence of good road, rail and air transport networks. Offices are also set up in the main cities of Shenzhen and Shanghai for what respondents called 'administrative convenience' in terms of access to the company's other resources such as ships (when at port) and offices (in Hong Kong).

It was also interesting to identify the propensity of some companies to invest in the underdeveloped regions of China such as Xinhua, Chongqing and Wuhan. This interest was declared despite the lack of transport infrastructure in these rather remote parts of the country. It was felt however, that these areas present opportunities for long-term development and could provide windfall returns after a period of 5-10 years. On the basis of this finding it may be postulated that the location decision may be associated with long-term strategic factors, something that has not been examined widely in the literature.

The findings of the study are consistent with those by Li (1993) who found that port cities are able to attract a relatively larger amount of foreign investment. It is only natural that special economic zones, established commercial centres and open cities will be preferred for foreign investment as they tend to reduce the uncertainty associated with FDI and take advantage of the privileges that these areas offer (see Eiteman, 1990). Foreign investors tend to favour locations with an established industrial base and well-developed physical infrastructure (Head and Ries, 1996; Henderson, 1986) and other region-specific political and socio-economic factors (Cho, 1988; Schroath *et al.*, 1993) as well as control on other company resources (Chen, 1996).

Modes of Market Entry and Internalisation

The major market entry modes utilised in the Chinese market by the companies participating in this research include formation of agency offices, wholly owned subsidiaries (WOSs) and contractual joint ventures (CJVs). Most companies preferred WOSs.

There was one case where CJV with a national express company was preferred. The foreign company performed the major management role in the joint venture. This form of market entry was preferred because of the legal requirement of joining with a local company. Although some advantages like knowledge of the local market accrued, there have been more problems registered in this partnership due to differences in management style, culture, facilities and the staff training system.

Another company initially opted to form agency offices because of government restrictions with regard to licensing for a WOS. In entering the Chinese market, the particular company first established agencies in the country and later converted those to WOSs following application and approval by the Chinese authorities. It was suggested that WOSs confer more substantive advantages to the company when compared to joint ventures or agencies. In their pioneering study on foreign market entry, Stopford and Wells (1972) argue that the more experience the MNE has in the host country, the more likely the firm will seek WOS, rather than joint ventures, as the mode of entry.

According to the interviewees it is easier to control, operate and manage WOSs by a head-office. The implementation of company policies among the branches is more effective, unlike joint ventures that suffer from problems of co-ordination. Wholly owned subsidiaries can exert control over the quality of service that can be delivered at an appropriate standard. It was held that the service provided by local companies or partners is unsatisfactory, whereas there is also the problem of sharing critical resources. There are clear indications that multinational shipping and logistics corporations prefer higher control modes of market entry.

When a multinational corporation invests in a foreign country, it has to consider the level of resource commitments in that particular domain. In other words the MNE has to consider the amount of investment in transaction-specific assets. Transaction-specific assets are non-re-deployable physical and human investments that are specialised and unique to a task (Williamson, 1985). Other authors claim that when host country risk is high, foreign investors will favour entry modes that involve relatively low resource commitments (Kim and Hwang, 1992). This means they tend to avoid WOSs or a high level of ownership in equity joint ventures. In the case of shipping and logistics multinationals in China, the important issues are that companies enter for the long-term and prefer to commit resources to this respect, particularly as risks have been decreasing due to the open door policy and the adoption of market principles by China. In addition the issue of control of critical resources and internalisation tends to favour WOSs.

Barriers to Entry

There was a general consensus among the interviewees that barriers to entry and operation in China still exist. One company faced a number of barriers prior to entry but also recurring problems during the period of operation in China. Prior to entry there was a complex and time consuming process of approval before the government and local authorities were satisfied in granting an entry licence. Some companies in the logistics industry have waited for two years before they could establish a subsidiary even in a big city like Shanghai. Despite the 'open door policy' companies came to realise that it was quite difficult to establish a company in China, particularly WOSs, which might take up to five years after the establishment of an equity joint venture with a local partner. Official licences granted by the Chinese Ministry of Communications are required before operations can commence. Some companies have official licences and have already established WOSs, something that gives them operational and strategic advantages over current competitors and potential new entrants.

Despite the attractiveness and the reforms that have been taking place in China a number of impediments have also been encountered by the companies. The first issue involves the bureaucracy that is associated with administrative procedures, inefficiencies in the co-ordination of government departments, unclear or contradictory laws and the uncertainty arising therefrom. In addition it seems that post-approval monitoring and evaluation mechanisms are weak. The result is again friction between the foreign investors and the interests of local investors and the host country. While a number of tax incentives are granted to foreign affiliates, domestic enterprises enjoy preferential treatment such as easy access to loans and low-priced raw materials. This causes unfair competition and market distortions and may be looked upon as an impediment to foreign investment.

Interviewees expressed the opinion that despite the open door policy, the Chinese market is not as open as other free market economies. There are more restrictions to foreign investors compared to local investors. Chinese laws regarding logistics are ambiguous and vague. There is a lack of complete and clear guidelines to logistics service providers. Foreign ocean carriers have to set up joint venture operations with Chinese companies in order to operate intermodal and logistics functions. In addition the implementation of customer procedures is complicated and the transport infrastructure facilities are below international standards.

It is also difficult to decide upon the best time for making the investment, whereas competition from local companies and other foreign entrants can be quite stiff, particularly as new entrants have to take some time in adapting to the new environment. This raises the issue of timing market entry, which will depend on external factors but also on the company's strategic orientation.

One of the main barriers to the conduct of smooth operations seems to be communication with government departments. It was felt that the traditional structure of government in China is complex and bureaucratic something that makes it difficult to tackle problems faced by private enterprises swiftly. One company found itself working towards the development of a special *guanxi* relationship with government departments as a means towards solving the problems faced. Trading practices in China are also of concern to logistics companies. In particular interviewees seem to be concerned with the existence of a black market where vast sums of money are being lost to rogue traders and the inability of the government to take decisive action against such practices.

Policy and Research Implications

Policy Implications

A number of suggestions in relation to policy formulation for attracting foreign logistics companies in China may be put forward. A general recommendation that can be made is the further encouragement for FDI in China's shipping and logistics industries by a concerted effort directed at reducing the restrictions that may exist in the path of foreign multinationals. Investment in transport and logistics will improve efficiency and lower distribution costs thus attracting a host of other potential investors from the manufacturing and retail sectors.

Under the current system, it seems that the government tries to encourage FDI on one hand through the open door policy and tax concessions and incentives, but provides substantial barriers on the other hand by delaying/rejecting the formation of WOS. According to internalisation theory, this may be one of the major reasons accounting for discouraging FDI and defeating the purposes of the open door policy itself. The government seems to place greater emphasis on the control of the operations of multinational enterprises as a means of bolstering the competitiveness of local and state-owned companies and encouraging the transfer of technology and knowledge. However, such transfers have not been occurring to the expected level (Kamath, 1990) for the reasons suggested by internalisation theory (Yelpaala, 1985; Rugman, 1980). Competition between FDI and state-owned enterprises seems to be a deterring factor in realising the full benefits of FDI in China (see Branstetter and Feenstra, 1999). It must be noted, however, that local ownership and control (which is evidently pursued) is not essential as long as foreign ownership and control is accompanied by the appropriate policies resulting in distributive equities in the private sector and social benefits from FDI, which are the sought after results. Ownership and control to foreign multinationals through a relaxed policy in the formation of WOS should be encouraged. In conjunction there must be appropriate legislation to ensure that such ownership and control does not result in monopoly profits, manipulation of the host country, or denationalisation.

In addition, foreign investors in shipping and logistics would welcome a more transparent legal system and less of the hasty and retrospective legislation. *Guanxi* relationships seem to play a significant role in the smooth operation of multinational shipping and logistics corporations. Sanyal and Guvenli (2000) also identified the importance of relationships with government departments for the achievement of foreign companies' objectives in China. On a related aspect, Wei (2000) goes so far as to suggest that corruption and red tape problems are important deterring factors that make China an under-achiever as a host of FDI. Qualified and competent labour supply also seems to pose a problem and investment in education can increase the attractiveness to foreign investors.

The problems identified by the research participants indicate limitations in incentive policies that will specifically encourage FDI in the shipping and logistics contexts. It is suggested in the general literature that policy makers should identify the bundle of resources, capital, technology and labour associated with encouraging FDI and develop complementary policies to enhance its total incentive package. There is a need for identifying industry-specific factors in order to encourage FDI in shipping and logistics. More specific shipping and transportation policies include taxation, facilitation of trade through reduction in quotas on imports and exports and customs policies. The tax system is problematic, vague and difficult to understand. More importantly for companies with presence in various provinces there are wide variations with different tax rates applying in different locations, which increase the complexity of the system. Quotas on imports and exports are too tight and customs procedures themselves extremely complex and time consuming. Companies have to spend vast sums of money and time to handle the voluminous amount of paper documentation. The customs system also changes quite rapidly and quite significantly. The customs system should be unified and rationalised across China. In this way carriers will find it easier and more convenient to transport cargoes between ports and cities in China.

Notwithstanding the tax advantages to foreign firms, domestic firms seem to enjoy preferential treatment (see Zhan, 1993). The functioning of multinational enterprises is based on the principle of internalisation. To the extent that discriminatory practices against foreign firms exist, then the full benefits of FDI may not be realised. The government should not only eliminate such practices but also actively encourage multinational enterprise FDI by subsidising the search costs associated with it such as information gathering and dissemination.

Shipping and logistics multinationals may be classified as market seekers under the Behrman (1972) typology. Market seekers will be attracted by market size but also by the potential accessibility to the market. To ensure market accessibility, the development of transport, logistics and port infrastructure is of the essence in China. There would be no point investing in a region or location that lacks the infrastructure to ensure cargo transportation as well as the superstructure for information dissemination, which is of the essence in logistics management.

Limitations and Research Implications

This study has implications for further research in the area. Inevitably, it also suffers from some limitations that need to be acknowledged. One limitation of this study it its cross-sectional nature. Sun *et al.* (2002) suggested that the determinants for FDI change over time. It will be therefore, useful to replicate the results of this study through empirical examination of the justification-oriented research hypotheses and that can be developed from the results herewith. In addition, the fact that the case-study approach has been adopted means that statistical generalisation and aggregate results over the whole population of MNEs investing in China cannot be attained. Of course, this was not the objective. The outcomes of this exploratory study reveal factors that can be the subject of justification-oriented research hypotheses in the context of motives, entry modes and ownership and location of shipping and logistics multinationals investing in China.

The motives for entering China include the size of the market and the potential it presents for logistics business and on current evidence, may not be related to cost-saving factors. According to the qualitative results from this study, market size, economic growth and increase in trade are positively related to FDI by shipping and logistics multinationals. FDI is also positively related to policies that promote internalisation. Multinational shipping and logistics corporations are also motivated by competitors' actions and FDI may be undertaken pro-actively to pre-empt similar moves of competitors or to match previous strategic moves of competitors.

Wholly owned subsidiaries are preferred as the mode of entry. This provides support for internalisation theory and opportunities for empirical investigation in the multinational shipping and logistics context.

In terms of location, justification-oriented research hypotheses may be put forward with regard to the propensity for locating in SEZs, open cities and port cities and the influence of distance between consumption and production nodes, the level of risk and uncertainty and proximity to administrative centres such as Beijing, Shanghai and Hong Kong.

One of the limitations that Sun *et al.* (2002) acknowledge for their study is that they do not consider differences between industrial sectors with the resulting implication that aggregate data may conceal important factors within industries. It is therefore, important that industrial sectors are considered on a case-by-case basis as a means for identifying richer, industry-specific factors. Hence, the contribution of this study and the case-study methodology adopted.

Conclusion

This paper provides an initial attempt to study issues in foreign direct investment of shipping and logistics multinationals in China. Despite the contribution of ocean shipping and logistics to international trade and world economic development, the multinational corporations of the industry have been rarely subjected to scientific scrutiny as to their international business practices in general and market entry strategies in particular. China undoubtedly presents vast opportunities for shipping and logistics multinationals, but also serious challenges for the companies as well as the policy-makers. The FDI literature and internalisation theory in particular provide ample opportunity for developing a framework to explore the patterns, obstacles, strategies and policies adopted by the corporations and governments. In the context of this study, it is important to note that the interests of foreign investors and host country may be equally served without social, private or state-owned enterprise costs. In addition to the policy implications that this qualitative study reveals, it also provides conceptual inferences that can be used for the development of justification-oriented research hypotheses. This can lead to replication and further development of theory as well as specific policy implications.

References

Agarwal, S. and Ramaswami, S.N. (1992) Choice of Foreign Market Entry Mode: Impact of Ownership, Location and Internalisation Factors, *Journal of International Business Studies*, 23, 1, 1-27.

Aharoni, Y. (1966) *The Foreign Investment Decision Process*, Cambridge, Massachusetts: Harvard University Press.

Aliber, R.A. (1970) A Theory of Foreign Direct Investment, in Kindleberger, C. (ed.), *The International Corporation,* Cambridge: The MIT Press, 17-34.

Anderson, E. and Coughlan, A.T. (1987) International Marketing Entry and Expansion Via Independent or Integrated Channels of Distribution, *Journal of Marketing*, 51, 1, 71-82.

Anderson, E. and Gatignon, H. (1986) Modes of Foreign Market Entry: a Transaction-cost Analysis and Propositions, *Journal of International Business Studies*, 17, 3, 1-26.

Anderson, E. and Weitz, B. (1986) Make or Buy Decisions: a Framework for Analysing Vertical Integration Issues in Marketing, *Sloan Management Review*, 27, Spring, 3-19.

Baek, H.Y. and Kwok, C.C.Y. (2002) Foreign Exchange Rates and the Corporate Choice of Foreign Entry Mode, *International Review of Economics and Finance*, 11, 1-21.

Balasubramanyan, V.N., Salisu, M. and Sapsford, D. (1996) Foreign Direct Investment and Growth in EP and IS Countries, *Economic Journal*, 106, 92-105.

Bauerschmidt, A., Sullivan, D. and Gillespie, K. (1985) Common Factors Underlying Barriers to Export: Studies in the US Paper Industry, *Journal of International Business Studies*, 16, Fall, 111-123.

Behrman, J.N. (1972) *The Role of International Companies in Latin America: Autos and Petrochemicals*, Lexington, Massachusetts Lexington Books.

Blomstrom, M., Lipsey, R. and Zejan, M. (1992) *What Explains Developing Country Growth*, NBER Working Paper No. 4132.

Boddewyn, J.J., Halbrich, M.B. and Perry, A.C. (1986) Service Multinationals: Conceptualisation, Measurement and Theory, *Journal of International Business Studies*, 17, Fall, 1-26.

Borensztein, E., De Gregorio, J. and Lee, J-W. (1998) How Does Foreign Direct Investment Affect Economic Growth? *Journal of International Economics*, 45, 115-135.

Branstetter, L. and Feenstra, R. (1999) *Trade and Foreign Direct Investment in China: a Political Economy Approach*, NBER Working Paper No. 7100.

Brewer, T.L. (1993) Government Policies, Market Imperfections, and Foreign Direct Investment, *Journal of International Business Studies*, 24, 101-120.

Buckley, P.J. (1988) The Limits of Explanation: Testing the Internalisation Theory of the Multinational Enterprise, *Journal of International Business Studies*, 19, 2, 181-193.

Buckley, P.J. and Casson, M.C. (1976) *The Future of the Multinational Enterprise*, London: Macmillan.

Buckley, P.J. and Casson, M.C. (1985) *The Economic Theory of the Multinational Enterprise: Selected Papers*, London, Macmillan.

Business Asia (1994) Constricted Arteries, January 17, 26, 2, China Supplement, 4-5.

Cantwell, J. (1991) A Survey of Theories of International Production, in C. Pitelis and R. Sugden (eds), *The Nature of the Transnational Firm*, (16-63), London: Routledge.

Caves, R.E. (1971) International Corporations: the Industrial Economics of Foreign Investments, *Economica*, 38, 1-27.

Caves, R.E. (1982) *Multinational Enterprise and Economic Analysis*, New York: Cambridge University Press.

Cavusgil, S.T. (1980) On the Internationalisation Process of Firms, *European Research*, 8, 6, 273-281.

Chang, S-J. and Rosenzweig, P.M. (2001) The Choice of Entry Mode in Sequential Foreign Direct Investment, *Strategic Management Journal*, 22, 747-776.

Chen, C.H. (1996) Regional Determinants of Foreign Direct Investment in Mainland China, *Journal of Economic Studies*, 23, 2, 18-30.

Chen, C., Chang, L. and Zhang, Y. (1995) The Role of Foreign Direct Investment in China's Post-1978 Economic Development, *World Development*, 23, 4, 691-703.

Cheng, L.K. and Kwan, Y.K. (2000) What Are the Determinants of the Location of Foreign Direct Investment? The Chinese Experience, *Journal of International Economics*, 51, 379-400.

China Statistics (2000) *A Statistical Survey of China*, Beijing: China Statistical Information and Consultancy Services Centre.

Cho, K.R. (1988) Determinants of Intra-Firm Trade: a Search for a Theoretical Framework, *The International Trade Journal*, 3, 2, 167-185.

Chung, W. (2001) Mode, Size, and Location of Foreign Direct Investments and Industry Markups, *Journal of Economic and Organisation*, 45, 185-211.

Coughlan, A.T. (1985) Competition and Cooperation in Marketing Channel Choice: Theory and Application, *Marketing Science*, 4, 2, 110-129.

Cushman, D.O. (1987) The Effects of Real Wages and Labour Productivity on Foreign Direct Investment, *Southern Economic Journal*, 54, July, 174-185.

Davidson, W.H. (1982) *Global Strategic Management*, New York: John Wiley and Sons.

Davidson, W.H. and McFeteridge, D.G. (1985) Key Characteristics in the Choice of International Technology Transfer Mode, *Journal of International Business Studies*, 16, 3, 5-22.

Dees, S. (1998) Foreign Direct Investment in China: Determinants and Effects, *Economics of Planning*, 31, 2, 175-194.

De Gregorio, J. (1992) Economic Growth in Latin America, *Journal of Development Economics*, 39, 58-84.

Dunning, J. (1980) Toward an Eclectic Theory of International Production: Some Empirical Tests, *Journal of International Business Studies*, 11, Spring/Summer, 9-31.

Dunning, J. (1988a) The Eclectic Paradigm of International Production: a Restatement and Some Possible Extensions, *Journal of International Business Studies*, 19, 1, 1-31.

Dunning, J. (1988b) *Explaining International Production*, Boston Massachusetts Unwin Hyman.

Dunning, J. (1993) *Multinational Enterprises and the Global Economy*, New York: Addison-Wesley.

Dunning, J. (1997) *Governments, Globalization and International Business*, Oxford: Oxford University Press.

Dunning, J. (2000) *Regions, Globalization and the Knowledge-based Economy*, Oxford: Oxford University Press.

Eisenhardt, K.M. (1989) Building Theory From Case Study Research, *Academy of Management Review*, 14, 4, 532-550.

Eisenhardt, K.M. (1995) Building Theories From Case Study Research. In Huber, G. and Van de Ven, A. (eds), *Longitudinal Field Research Methods*, Thousand Oaks: Sage Publications, 532-550.

Eiteman, D.K. (1990) American Executives' Perceptions of Negotiating Joint Ventures with the People's Republic of China: Lessons Learned, *Columbia Journal of World Business*, Winter, 59-67.

Erramilli, M.K. (1991) The Experience Factor in Foreign Market Entry Behaviour of Service Firms, *Journal of International Business Studies*, 22, 3, 479-501.

Erramilli, M.K. and Rao, C.P. (1990) Choice of Foreign Market Entry Modes by Service Firms: Role of Market Knowledge, *Management International Review*, 30, 2, 135-150.

Erramilli, M.K. and Rao, C.P. (1993) Service Firms' International Market Entry Mode Choice: a Modified Transaction Cost Analysis Approach, *Journal of Marketing*, 57, 3, 19-38.

Findlay, R. (1978) Relative Backwardness, Direct Foreign Investment, and the Transfer of Technology: a Simple Dynamic Model, *Quarterly Journal of Economics*, 92, 1-16.

Foreign Investment in China (1996) *China Foreign-Invested Enterprises Association*, 41, 20.

Gatignon, H. and Anderson, E. (1987) *The Multinational Corporation's Degree of Control Over Foreign Subsidiaries: an Empirical Test of a Transaction Cost Explanation*, Report Number 87-103, Cambridge, Massachusetts Marketing Science Institute.

Gomes-Casseres, B. (1990) Firm Ownership Preferences and Host Government Restrictions: an Integrated Approach, *Journal of International Business Studies*, 21, 1, 1-21.

Goodnow, J.D. (1985) Developments in International Mode of Entry Analysis, *International Marketing Review*, Autumn, 17-30.

Goodnow, J.D. and Hansz, J.H. (1972) Environmental Determinants of Overseas Market Entry Strategies, *Journal of International Business Studies*, 3, Spring, 33-60.

Grosse, R. and Behrman, N.J. (1992) Theory in International Business, *Transnational Corporations*, 1, 1, 93-126.

Grub, P.G., Lin, J.H. and Xia, M. (1990) Foreign Investment in China: a Study and Analysis of Factors Influencing the Attitudes and Motivations of US Firms, in Neghandi, A. R. and Schran, P. (eds), *China and India: Foreign Investment and Economic Relations*, Research in International Business Relations, 4, 83-99, JAI Press Inc.

Head, K. and Ries, J. (1996) Inter-city Competition for Foreign Investment: Static and Dynamic Effects of China's Incentive Areas, *Journal of Urban Economics*, 40, 38-46.

Hein, S. (1992) Trade Strategy and the Dependency Hypothesis: a Comparison of Policy, Foreign Investment and Economic Growth in Latin America and East Asia, *Economic Development and Cultural Change*, 40, 3, 495-521.

Henderson, J.V. (1986) Efficiency of Resource Usage and City Size, *Journal of Urban Economics*, 19, 47-70.

Hennart, J-F. and Park, Y. (1993) Greenfield versus Acquisition: the Strategy of Japanese Investors in the United States, *Management Science*, 39, 9, 1054-1070.

Hennart, J-F. and Reddy, S. (1997) The Choice Between Mergers/Acquisitions and Joint Ventures: the Case of Japanese Investors in The United States, *Strategic Management Journal*, 18, 1, 1-12.

Hymer, S.H. (1960) *The International Operations of National Firms: a Study of Direct Foreign Investment*, Cambridge Massachusetts MIT Press.

Hymer, S.H. (1976) The International Operations of National Firms: a Study of Direct Foreign Investment, Cambridge Massachusetts MIT Press.

Johanson, J. and Vahlne, J. (1977) The Internationalisation Process of the Firm: a Model of Knowledge Development and Increasing Foreign Commitments, *Journal of International Business Studies*, Spring/Summer, 23-32.

Jun, K.W. and Singh, H. (1996) The Determinants of Foreign Direct Investment in Developing Countries, *Transnational Corporations*, 5, 2, 67-105.

Kamath, S.J. (1994) Foreign Direct Investment in a Centrally Planned Developing Economy: the Chinese Case, *Economic Development and Cultural Change*, 39, October, 107-130.

Kim, W.C. and Hwang, P. (1992) Global Strategy and Multinationals' Entry Mode Choice, *Journal of International Business Studies*, 23, 1, 29-53.

Kimura, Y. (1989) Firm Specific Strategic Advantages and Foreign Direct Investment Behaviour of Firms: the Case of Japanese Semi-Conductor Firms, *Journal of International Business Studies*, 20, Summer, 296-314.

Kindleberger, C.P. (1969) *American Business Abroad*, New Haven, Connecticut Yale University Press.

Kogut, B. and Singh, H. (1988) The Effect of National Culture on the Choice of Entry Mode, *Journal of International Business Studies*, 19, 3, 411-432.

Larimo, J. (1995) The Foreign Direct Investment Decision Process: Case Studies of Different Types of Decision Processes in Finnish Firms, *Journal of Business Research*, 33, 1, 25-55.

Lecraw, D.J. (1984) Bargaining Power, Ownership, and Profitability of Trans-National Corporations in Developing Countries, *Journal of International Business Studies*,15, 2, 27-43.

Leonard-Barton, D. (1990) A Dual Methodology For Case Studies: Synergistic Use of a Longitudinal Single Site with Replicated Multiple Sites, *Organisation Science*, 1, 1, 248-266.

Levis, M. (1979) Does Political Instability in Developing Countries Affect Foreign Investment Flow? An Empirical Examination, *Management International Review*, 19, 59-68.

Li, J. and Guisinger, S. (1991) Comparative Business Failures of Foreign-Controlled Firms in The United States, *Journal of International Business Studies*, 22, 2, 209-224.

Li, N. (1993), Port Construction Stepped Up to Relieve Bottlenecks, *Beijing Review*, 36 35, 12-16.

Liu, X., Wang, C. and Wei, Y. (2001) Causal Links Between Foreign Direct Investment and Trade in China, *China Economic Review*, 12, 190-202.

Lucas, R. (1993) On the Determinants of Direct Foreign Investment: Evidence from East And Southeast Asia, *World Development*, 21, 3, 391-406.

Luo, Y. (1998) *International Investment Strategies in the People's Republic of China*, Aldershot: Ashgate.

Luo, Y. and Tan, J. J. (1997) How Much Does Industry Structure Impact Foreign Direct Investment in China? *International Business Review*, 6, 4, 337-359.

Mudambi, R. (1995) The MNE Investment Location Decision: Some Empirical Evidence, *Managerial and Decision Economics*, 16, 249-257.

OECD (1998) *Foreign Direct Investment and Economic Development – Lessons from Six Emerging Economies,* Organisation for Economic Co-operation and Development: Paris.

Oxelheim, L., Randoy, T. and Stonehill, A. (2001) On the Treatment of Finance-Specific Factors within the OLI Paradigm, *International Business Review*, 10, 381-398.

Remenyi, D., Williams, B., Money, A. and Swartz, E. (1998) *Doing Research in Business and Management*, London: Sage Publications.

Root, F.R. (1987) *Foreign Market Entry Strategies*, New York: AMACOM.

Rugman, A. (1980) Internalisation as a General Theory of Foreign Investment: a Reappraisal of the Literature, *Weltwirtschaftliches Archiv*, 116, 365-379.

Rugman, A. (1981) *Inside the Multinationals: the Economics of Internal Markets*, New York: Columbia University Press.

Sabi, M. (1988) An Application of the Theory of Foreign Direct Investment to Multinational Banking in LDCs, *Journal of International Business Studies*, 19, Fall, 433-448.

Sanyal, R.N. and Guvenli, T. (2000) Relations Between Multinational Firms and Host Governments: the Experience of American-Owned Firms in China, *International Business Review*, 9, 119-134.

Schneider, F. and Frey, B.S. (1985) Economic and Political Determinants of Foreign Direct Investment, *World Development*, 13, 161-175.

Schroath, F.W. Hu, M.Y. and Chen, H. (1993) Country-of-Origin Effects of Foreign Investments in the People's Republic of China, *Journal of International Business Studies*, 24, 277-290.

Speece, M.W. and Kawahara, Y. (1995) Transportation in China in the 1990s, *International Journal of Physical Distribution and Logistics Management*, 25, 8, 53-71.

Stopford, J.M. and Wells, L.T. (1972) *Managing the Multinational Enterprise*, New York: Basic Books.

Sun, Q., Tong, W. and Yu, Q. (2002) Determinants of Foreign Direct Investment Across China, *Journal of International Money and Finance*, 21, 79-113.

Ta, H-P., Choo, H-L. and Sum, C-C. (2000) Transportation Concerns of Foreign Firms in China, *International Journal of Physical Distribution and Logistics Management*, 30, 1, 35-54.

Tallman, S.B. and Shenkar, O. (1994) A Managerial Decision Model of International Co-Operative Venture Formation, *Journal of International Business Studies*, 25, 1, 91-113.

Tatoglu, E. and Glaister, K. W. (1998) An Analysis of the Motives for Western FDI in Turkey, *International Business Review*, 7, 203-230.

Terpstra, V. and Yu, C-M. (1988) Determinants of Foreign Investment of US Advertising Agencies, *Journal of International Business Studies*, 19, Spring, 33-46.

Vernon, R. (1966) International Investment and Multinational Trade in the Product Cycle, *Quarterly Journal of Economics*, 80, 190-207.

Voss, C., Tsikriktsis, N. and Frohlich, M. (2002) Case Research in Operations Management, *International Journal of Operations Management*, 22, 2, 195-219.

Wang, J-Y. (1990) Growth, Technology Transfer and the Long-Run Theory of International Capital Movements, *Journal of International Economics*, 29, 255-271.

Wei, S.-J. (2000) *Can China and India Double Their Inward Foreign Direct Investment?* NBER Working Paper.

Wheeler, D. and Mody, A. (1992) International Investment Location Decisions, the Case of US firms, *Journal of International Economics*, 33, 57-76.

Williamson, O.E. (1975) *Markets and Hierarchies*, New York: The Free Press.

Williamson, O.E. (1985) *The Economic Institutions of Capitalism*, New York: The Free Press.

Woodcock, C.P., Beamish, P.W. and Makino, S. (1994) Ownership-based Entry Mode Strategies and International Performance, *Journal of International Business Studies*, 25, 2, 253-273.

Wu, Y. (2000) Measuring the Performance of Foreign Direct Investment: a Case Study of China, *Economic Letters*, 66, 143-150.

Wu, X. and Strange, R. (2000) The Location of Foreign Insurance Companies In China, *International Business Review*, 9, 383-398.

Yelpaala, K. (1985) In Search of Effective Policies for Foreign Direct Investment: Alternatives to Tax Incentive Policies, *Northwestern Journal of International Law and Business*, 7, 208-266.

Yin, R. (1994) *Case Study Research*, Beverly Hills, CA: Sage Publications

Zang, X. (1995) Foreign Direct Investment in China's Economic Development, in *The New Wave of Foreign Direct Investment in Asia*, Nomura Research Institute and Institute of Southeast Asian Studies.

Zhan, X.J. (1993) The Role of Foreign Direct Investment in Market-Oriented Reforms and Economic Development: The Case of China, *Transnational Corporations*, 2, 3, 121-148.

Zhang, Q. and Felmingham, B. (2001) The Relationship Between Inward Direct Foreign Investment and China's Provincial Export Trade, *China Economic Review*, 12, 82-99.

Zhao, H. and Zhu, G. (1998) Determinants of Ownership Preference of International Joint Ventures: New Evidence from Chinese Manufacturing Industries, *International Business Review*, 7, 569-589.

11 Logistics Development in the Port of Shanghai

Li Bao and Richard Gray
Institute of Marine Studies
University of Plymouth
Plymouth, United Kingdom

Introduction

Throughout the world, port authorities and shipping companies are reacting to developments in logistics and supply chain management. The Port of Shanghai needs to adapt to a situation in which a seaport is not only part of a transport chain, but also a key component in global supply chains. Many multinational corporations (MNCs) have established manufacturing and sales divisions in China over the last two decades, but there has not been an equivalent advance in the basic infrastructure of logistics, such as transport and warehousing capacity. Indeed, it has become increasingly difficult for manufacturers and marketers in China to expedite products efficiently. A survey of over 200 United States exporters to China claimed that poor performance of local suppliers and carriers in China are basic concerns and create significant barriers to international operations (Carter *et al*, 1997). China has lagged behind other countries in applying the concepts of logistics and supply chain management. In this context, there is a lack of experience in generating strategies for the supply of logistics services in the Port of Shanghai. This paper examines the lessons for Shanghai from the experience of logistics services offered by world-class port authorities or operators. Furthermore, a comparison is made with other major ports in competition with Shanghai, and which have the ability to transfer cargo to and from China.

The Impact of Global Change

Changes in the global market environment, of which ports are a part, have taken place for several reasons. In line with increased globalisation, MNCs are sourcing their products globally, assisted by deregulation and technological innovation. Simultaneously, there has been the acceptance of integrated supply chain management based on sophisticated logistics practices. Partly in reaction to this, international freighting companies are merging or forming close associations both horizontally and vertically. For example, shipping lines have formed global alliances, and there has been an increase in transport companies offering comprehensive integrated logistics services. Ports have also had to react to this changing situation by competing for the role of hub ports in hub-and-spoke container networks and by developing as logistics centres.

Since China adopted widespread reforms and introduced an open-door policy it has become part of this changing scene. Over the past two decades there has been an increase in China's merchandise exports from US\$ 18.9 billion in 1980 to US\$ 249.21 billion in 2000 (World Trade Organisation, 2001). Shipping has played an important role in China's economic development, which in turn has given its seaports opportunities for development. China's shipping policy in the contemporary era can be broadly divided into the two periods of 1949 to 1978 and from 1979 to the present. The second period has been a gradual change towards an open policy (Sun and Zhang, 1999). Figure 11.1 illustrates that this has led to a remarkable increase in container throughput in China from 1980 to 2000.

However, changes in global markets and supply chains have forced many seaports to change their practices, and Chinese seaports will also have to adapt, not only by improving productivity and efficiency, but also by performing new functions as logistics centres. As the largest seaport in mainland China, the Port of Shanghai should not only develop its deep water container terminal, but also examine its potential for world class logistics services.

The Potential for Logistics Centres

Globalisation, together with containerisation, facilitates the development of integrated logistics, and encourages the establishment of logistics service providers. Integrated logistics services require not just transhipment but also a range of product or customer-orientated logistics services (European Conference of Ministers of Transport, 1997, p. 24). A logistics centre can offer all the key components of logistics (transport, inventory management, storage, materials handling, and order processing). It can provide industrial companies with a central distribution location, not only for transhipment, consolidation and break bulk, but also for various forms of so-called value-added logistics services such as postponement, reverse logistics, packaging and labelling, etc.

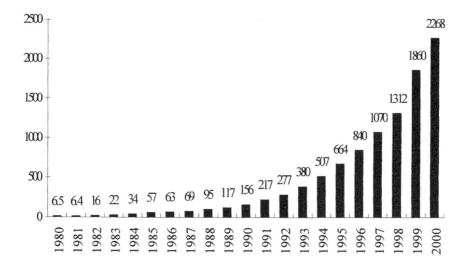

Source: (Gao Huijun, 2000, p.29)

Figure 11.1: 1980-2000 Total Container Throughput in China (10,000TEU)

Ports are ideally suited to become logistics centres. From the integrated logistics standpoint, ports are important strategic points in global production, trade and transport, and play a crucial role in the global supply chain. A port is not only an interchange point between sea and land, but also an information centre, and even a suitable location for some elements of production. A port is a node for the flows of goods, information and human resources. In many cases a port has evolved from purely a transport interchange point to a logistics centre, a transhipment hub, a distripark, part of an intermodal transport system, and a teleport (Luo, 2001).

The concept of a distripark is being adopted by many ports which have turned themselves into trade distribution centres. A distripark is a trading area, where industrial companies are able to open distribution centres and take advantage of nearby port infrastructure and hinterland. This enables companies to maintain closer control of their inventories so that 'just-in-time' delivery systems can be operated, and inventory levels can be kept low. Distriparks are also ideal locations for value-added logistics (VAL) services. VAL has been described as a combination of logistical and light industrial activities undertaken to finalise a product (Buck Consultants International, 1997). Ideally, this happens as late as possible in the logistics chain, preferably in a warehouse shortly before sending the product to its final destination. This process is based on the 'principle of postponement', where a generic stock is maintained for as long as possible in the supply chain, thus reducing overall inventory levels. The activities are defined according to the amount of value added to the product or service. VAL activities cover a wide range of services such as labelling, making the product country or customer-specific, adding manuals and parts, creating new assortments of goods, breaking bulk, blending or mixing of products or liquids, final assembly, and repairs to products.

Other functions that can take place in a distripark include value-added services (VAS) such as managing the goods and information flow, insurance, customs clearance, order entry or staffing a help-desk. A distripark can also offer value-added facilities (VAF) including such services as equipment maintenance, renting and leasing, or cleaning facilities (World Bank, 2001).

Most of the above value-added functions can be performed within a port area, and the fact that they are available may encourage a port user to stay at a specific port, since it may be impossible or difficult to get a similar level of service elsewhere. Activities in a distripark are ideally supported by an intermodal transport network of road, rail, inland water, and air, ensuring a smooth and efficient interchange of cargo.

The Port of Shanghai

Shanghai, a port city, is located on the mid-east coast of China. In China, people describe its 1,800km coastal line as a bow, and the 6,300km

Yangtse River as an arrow, so the Port of Shanghai is where the bow and arrow meet. It is the largest multi-purpose port on the mainland of China and one of the leading ports in the world, occupying a total area of about 3,600km² and 240 km of shoreline consisting of the mouth of the Yangtse River, Huangpu River and the northern part of Hangzhou Bay (Shanghai Port Authority, 2000).

Since Shanghai began its container operations in 1978, the throughput of containers has grown dramatically from just over 30,000 TEU at the beginning of the 1980s, to 465,100 TEU in 1990 and 5,613,000 TEU in 2000 (Table 11.1). At the same time, Shanghai's ranking for container throughput among the world ports rose from 20th in 1995 to 6th in 2000 (Shou, 2000, p. 1). The throughput of containers in the port of Shanghai reached 6,000,000 TEU on the 12th of December 2001, with a total throughput in 2001 of 6.33 million TEU (Containerisation, 2002).

Table 11.1: Throughput of Containers in the Port of Shanghai 1990-2000 (000 TEU)

Year	Throughput (000TEU)	% Change
1990	456.1	-
1991	576.7	26.4
1992	730.5	26.7
1993	934.8	28.0
1994	1,199.0	28.3
1995	1,527.0	27.4
1996	1,970.0	29.0
1997	2,537.0	28.7
1998	3,066.0	20.9
1999	4,216.0	37.5
2000	5,613.0	33.1

Source: Adapted from (Guo, 2000, p17) and (Beddow, 2001, p. 93).

At present, container operations in Shanghai are divided into the two sectors of Shanghai Container Terminal (SCT) and Waigaoqiao area (WGQ) (Table 11.2). SCT, operated by HPH (Hutchison Port Holdings), consists of three terminals at Zhang Hua Bang, Jun Gong Lu and Bao Shan. WGQ is situated along the Pudong coastline between Shanghai and the East China Sea in a development zone regarded as the largest construction site in the world. It is aiming for a total quay length of 1800 metres and a total capacity of 1.2 million TEU (True, 2000).

Shanghai International Shipping Centre

Since adopting reform and an open-door policy, Shanghai's economy has been developing at a rapid pace. The municipal government seeks to develop Shanghai into an international economic, financial and trade centre and also a shipping centre. The strategy of establishing Shanghai as an international shipping centre stems from its location at the 'dragonhead' of the Yangtse delta. Accelerating the growth of maritime and port-related industries in the Yangtse river area should enable Shanghai to be a hub port with a much larger share of the Asia region's cargo than at present. As shown in Table 11.3, in 1998 about half of the Port of Shanghai's trade was from Shanghai foreign trade itself, and the rest was transhipment from the hinterland.

Table 11.2: Existing Container Terminals in Port of Shanghai (000 TEU)

Terminal		No. of Berths	Designed Throughput Capacity
SCT	Zhang Hua Bang	3	800
	Jun Gong Lu	4	650
	Bao Shan	3	250
WGQ	Phase I	3	600
	Phase II	4	600
TOTAL		**17**	**2,900**

Source: (Gu, 2000, p. 1).

To be a world-class shipping centre, the Port of Shanghai needs at least to possess the following features (Zhang, 2000, p.77):

- Deep water maritime facilities;
- An international container terminal capable of accommodating fifth and sixth generation container ships;
- A free-port system;
- Abundant cargo flow;
- A developed shipping market; and
- Highly efficient transport and distribution systems plus modern telecommunication/information exchange facilities.

Existing Limitations of the Port of Shanghai

As already stated, the Port of Shanghai has been one of the fastest growing ports in the world, and recently it has experienced a substantial growth rate, averaging over 30 per cent per year in the last three years. The cause of this growth is accelerated export demand, likely to be sustained following China's acceptance to the World Trade Organisation (WTO). However, Shanghai needs to develop significantly in order to cope with this growth.

Table 11.3: The Comparison of Shanghai Foreign Trade with Port of Shanghai Trade (US$ billion)

Year	1990	1992	1994	1996	1997	1998
Total of SPT[a]	7.341	9.157	15.867	22.263	24.764	31.440
Total of SFT[b]	17.289	25.154	36.242	52.870	58.683	63.640
SFT as % of SPT	43.0	38.8	43.8	42.1	42.2	49.4

Notes: [a] Total of Shanghai Port Trade, [b] Total of Shanghai Foreign Trade.
Source: (Qu & Han, 1999, p.15).

Despite continuing expansion of the WGQ area and productivity improvements at SCT, Shanghai's container throughput continues to exceed the intended terminal capacity. For instance, as shown in Table 11.4, in 1998 all of the container terminals in the Port of Shanghai exceeded their designed throughput capacity.

There are 20 major shipping lines in the world establishing branches in Shanghai and 16 ocean container transport routes calling at Shanghai. Cargo handled in Shanghai can be divided into four categories according to trades and shipping services (Guo, 2000, p.18):

- Ocean-international services mainly to USA and Europe;
- Short-sea international services mainly to Japan, Korea and South-east Asia;
- Coastal-domestic services to points along China's coastline; and
- River-domestic services to points in the lower part of the Yangtse River.

Among the above four categories of trade flows, the major foreign trade partners are Japan, the USA, Hong Kong, South Korea, and the EU.

In particular, the share of shipments to Europe and North America in the total trade of Shanghai is increasing. Nevertheless, Table 11.5 (showing the major liner operations on the Asia/North America route) illustrates that there are hardly any vessels with a capacity of more than 4,000 TEU calling at Shanghai, and this situation also applies to the Far East/Europe route. This means that, at present, the Port of Shanghai cannot be a hub port within the Far East region, and is therefore unlikely to increase its transhipment share in the container throughput of the region. In 1997, the percentage of international transhipment was more than 75 per cent in Singapore, over 60 per cent in Hong Kong and above 40 per cent in Rotterdam, but just 0.51 per cent in Shanghai (Cao, 2000, p. 25).

Table 11.4: The Over-quota of Designed Throughput Capacity (DTC) in Shanghai in 1998 (000 TEU)

Terminal		Berths	DTC	Throughput	Overquota	%
SCT	Zhang Hua Bang	3	800	916	116	14.5
	Jun Gong Lu	4	650	844	194	29.8
	Bao Shan	3	250	273	23	9.2
WGQ	Phase I	3	600	675	75	12.5

Source: (Shou, 2000, p.1).

Table 11.5 indicates that the two major limitations of the Port of Shanghai are lack of capacity and insufficient depth of water. To solve these problems, the Shanghai Port Authority has undertaken a joint venture to develop the port with terminal operators such as HPH, shipping lines such as COSCO and OOCL, and with a selection of other industries. This includes improving the productivity of the existing terminal, expanding the area of the same terminal, increasing the depth of the Yangtse River, and undertaking a feasibility study into the possibilities of building a new deep water container terminal.

Development of the Port of Shanghai

HPH (Hutchison Port Holding) operates SCT with three terminals at Zhang Hua Bang, Jun Gong Lu and Bao Shan providing a total berth length of 2,281 metres. The combined stacking capacity of the three terminals is 60,800 TEU, and handling capacity is 2.05m TEU, with a throughput of

2.6m TEU in 1999. To enable the terminal to achieve a much faster handling speed, HPH has invested heavily in new equipment and computer systems. At present, SCT has a total of 20 quay cranes and 54 rubber-tyred gantry cranes (RTGs), including two 50 tonne post-Panamax quayside cranes with twin-lift spreaders. In addition, SCT is planning to upgrade its capacity to a ground stacking capacity of 100,000 TEU (True, 2000; Fossey, 2000a; Hutchison Port Holdings, 2002).

Table 11.5: Major Lines Operations on Asia/North America Routes, 1st March 2001

Service operators	Ports of call	No. of vessels deployed	Capacity (nominal TEU)
Grand Alliance (NYK, OOCL, P&O, Hapag Lloyd)	*SSX* Long Beach, Kaohsiung, Hong Kong, Port Klang, Singapore, Yantian, Hong Kong, Long Beach	6	4,960-5,762
	JCX Los Angeles, Oakland, Vancouver, Seattle, Tokyo, Nagoya, Kobe, Hakarta, Shanghai, Kobe, Nakoya, Tokyo, Sendai, Los Angeles	6	2,897-2,990
Maersk Sealand TP6/AE5	Long Beach, Tacoma, Yokohama, Kobe, Kaohsiung, Hong Kong, Yantian, Tangjung Pelepas, European Ports, Salalah, Tangjung Pelepas, Yantian, Hong Kong, Long Beach	13	7,200
TP2	Long Beach, Oakland, Dutch Harbour, Yokohama, Nagoya, Busan, Naha, Hing Kong, Xiamen, Shanghai, Ningbo, Kwangyang, Busan, Long Beach	6	2,686

Table 11.5: concluded

New World Alliance (APL, Hyundai, MOL)	Los Angeles, Oakland, Tokyo, Nagoya, Shanghai, Kobe, Tokyo, Los Angeles,	5	2,826-2,890
PSW	Long Beach, Oakland, Tacoma, Busan, Kwangyang, Yantian, Hong Kong, Kaohsiung, Busan, Long Beach	5	5,551-6,400
United Alliance (Hanjin, Senator, Cho Yang) PDA	Long Beach, Oakland, Tokyo, Osaka, Busan, Hong Kong, Port Klang, Colombo, North European Ports, Singapore, Yantian, Hong Kong, Kaohsiung, Long Beach	12	5,302-5,744
CAX	Long Beach, Oakland, Busan, Kwangyang, Xingang, Shanghai, Busan, Long Beach	5	4,024
COSCO SEA	Long Beach, Seattle, Vancouver, Yokohama, Kobe, Shekou, Hong Kong, Yokohama, Long Beach	5	5,446
CES	Long Beach, Oakland, Yokohama, Hong Kong, Xiamen, Ningbo, Shanghai, Kobe, Nagoya, Long Beach	6	2,227-2,761
COSCO/K Line/Yong ming AEX	New York, Norfolk, Charleston, Tokyo, Kobe, Shanghai, Yantian, Hong Kong, New York	9	2,875-3,400

Source: extracted from Lloyd's Shipping Economist (2001), April, p.17-18).

Two phases of major development at the WGQ port area have increased the total length of container quay to 1,800m and capacity at the port to 1.2m TEU. However this is still not sufficient to satisfy the demand for container capacity. Under a third phase, the Shanghai Port Authority, HPH and COSCO have agreed to develop the terminal to add at least two more berths, resulting in a total capacity of 1.8m TEU. The preparation for a fourth phase has also taken place (True, 2000).

The depth of the mouth of the Yangtse River seriously restricts the expansion of the Port of Shanghai, which cannot handle fourth generation ships fully loaded because of draught restrictions in the Yangtse. The Shanghai municipal government and the port authority are now attending to this problem by deepening the navigational channel through the mouth of the Yangtse River, and the depth of water has increased from 7m to 8.5m. Nevertheless, the entire project to deepen the channel to 12.5m (14m at high tide) will take ten years at an estimated cost of $US 1.3 billion, and the second and third stages will be opened to foreign investment (True, 2000).

To become an international hub, Shanghai requires a 15m depth deep-water container terminal suitable for fifth and sixth generation container ships. There are four possible locations of terminals in central China, two at the mouth of the Yangtse River at Dayangshan and Xiaoyangshan, and two outside Shanghai at Qingdao, and Ningbo. A study is comparing the additional cost of trucking or water feeders to ports outside Shanghai against the high construction and operation costs of Yangshan and deepening the Yangtse River (Ashar, 2000). There is a feasibility study to build a huge, deep-water container terminal on the islands of Xiaoyangshan and Dayangshan in a group of partially inhabited islands in Hangzhou Bay, south of Shanghai. The project includes a 52-berth container terminal as well as a 32-km bridge to connect the islands to the mainland, with six lanes. The first phase will provide three to five container berths with a capacity of 2.5m TEU (True, 2000).

The Potential for Logistics Development in the Port of Shanghai

Juhel (1999) described the new role of ports at a logistics seminar in China in 1999:

> Nowadays, a port must offer efficient and reliable services to ships and cargo, including communication systems, documentation and Customs procedure, to allow the timely flow of goods through the transport chain which has, in fact, become a production chain. To assist in this flow, some countries have developed distribution or logistics centres in the port area, which is used for the storage, preparation and transformation of

cargo. Therefore, ports are no longer simply a place for cargo exchange but are a functional element in the dynamic logistics chains through which commodities and goods flow. An efficient transport system is also a pre-requisite to attract foreign direct investment. (Juhel, 1999, p.4)

Trade and industry require more sophisticated logistics service as demand grows for integrated logistics solutions instead of individual services, and, as stated earlier, it is inevitable that a port should be a vital node within the integrated supply chain. The Chinese government aims to establish Shanghai as an international shipping, trading and financial centre like those of Hong Kong and Singapore. However, even with its vast hinterland, the development of modern cargo handling facilities, and the creation of a satisfactory deep-water terminal, Shanghai is unlikely to become an international hub unless it is able to offer state-of-the-art logistics facilities.

China's Role in the Development of World Trade

China's economy is developing dramatically with an average annual growth rate of about 9.5 per cent from 1978 to 1999, and foreign trade has also increased rapidly (Transport Committee of Ningbo, 2000). China now makes a quarter of the world's toys, a third of its suitcases and handbags and an eighth of its footwear and clothing. China's entry to the WTO should assist such progress, and its GDP is likely to double between 2000 and 2010.

As the largest manufacturing, trading and consuming centre in China, Shanghai's economy has benefited from the reform and open-door policy, with the GDP of Shanghai increasing by nearly 400 per cent during the nine years up to 2000 (Figure 11.2).

The foreign trade of Shanghai has also increased dramatically. According to Shanghai Customs, the Port of Shanghai's trade had reached a record high of US$ 120 billion in 2001, up 10.2 per cent over 2000. Shanghai had taken a quarter of the previous year's national foreign trade volume. Of the total trade in 2001, imports through Shanghai amounted to US$ 52 billion and exports US$ 68 billion. Of the exports, the volume through the free trade zone is up 40 per cent (compared with an increase of 10.5 per cent for exports in general) (Shipping Gazette, 2002).

Billion US$

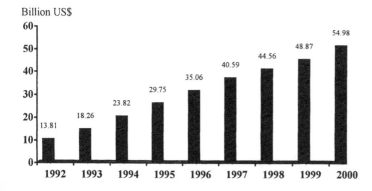

Source: Shanghai Statistics Bureau (2000).

Figure 11.2: The GDP of Shanghai in 1992-2000

The Transport and Communication System of the Port of Shanghai

The Port of Shanghai has reasonable transport connections by rail, inland water and road. It is connected to the inland provinces via the Yangtse River as far as Chongqing, approximately 2,400 km from Shanghai. The railway network consists of trunk lines connecting Beijing, Hangzhou and other major cities in China. The opening of the Shanghai-Kowloon railway shortened the travel time between Hong Kong and Shanghai to 29 hours. Moreover, the road links have been greatly improved in recent years, with highways linking Shanghai with Ningbo and Nanjing. For airfreight, there are the two largest airports in China, which form the hub of civil aviation in east China. One is Hongqiao Airport to the west of Shanghai, the other is Pudong Airport located to the east of Shanghai.

An EDI system is now being operated to speed up the customs procedure in the Port of Shanghai. The construction of a City Central Network and central networks for customs procedures, foreign trade, and harbour and aviation have been completed as part of an important project for Shanghai, *Skeleton of Shanghai Infor-Port Project* (Shanghai Informatization Office, 2000). Traditionally, customs authorities have had the role of protecting national borders and ensuring that duties are collected. The more modern approach is also to ensure that customs assist in facilitating trade. In 1999 a coalition of private companies, and the United States and Chinese customs services formed a public-private partnership called the Shanghai Model Port Project with the aim of converting Shanghai into a model modern customs centre. It should result in faster customs clearance and less paperwork, and will assist the Chinese customs in meeting WTO requirements (China Business Review, 2001).

Application of Logistics Strategies to the Port of Shanghai

To survive in the modern competitive environment, a seaport should become an integrated part of global supply chains. The application of logistics strategies is critical and Shanghai Port Authority needs to consider a number of key questions, based mainly on the advice of the World Bank (2001), when reviewing development strategies.

- What does the port of Shanghai want to become?
- In what maritime transport market environment is Shanghai operating?
- Which other ports have access to the hinterland market?
- Will future supply and demand for port services in the region be in balance?
- Where does Shanghai have a comparative advantage over its competitors?
- What actions can Shanghai take to attract and maintain customers?

Let us consider each of these questions.

What Does the Port of Shanghai Want to Become?

The objectives of the Port of Shanghai can be presented as a four-stage development.

- To become a regional hub in Eastern Asia;
- To set up logistics centres in the Port of Shanghai to meet customers' requirements for logistics services, and to strengthen the competitiveness of Shanghai;

- To become a controllable component in the improvement of the efficiency of transport logistics in China; and
- To integrate the port services with the other components of the global distribution network.

In What Maritime Transport Market Environment is Shanghai Operating?

Globalisation and containerisation have led to strategic alliances among major container shipping lines. Furthermore, some shipping liner companies have widened the scope of their functions to act as logistics service providers (LSPs). These developments have led to the formation of hub-and-spoke networks along the main sea routes, creating intense competition within the seaport market.

Which Other Ports Have Access to the Hinterland Market?

The Port of Shanghai is in fierce competition with neighbouring ports such as Kobe, Tokyo, Yokohama in Japan, and Busan (or Pusan) in South Korea. Shanghai will not be able to maintain a competitive position if its capacity does not meet the continuing demand for transhipment based on the growth of both container throughput and container vessel size (Cargo Systems, 2000).

Will Future Supply and Demand for Port Services in the Region be in Balance?

In 2000 China managed to achieve the status of the seventh largest trading nation with a trade surplus of US\$ 24.1 billion (China Statistical Data, 2002). A Reuters Asia report of 1st March 2002 quoted a Chinese Government estimate of economic growth of 7.3 per cent for 2001, the best in Asia, although some Western analysts claim that this could be overstated by 0.5 per cent to 1.0 per cent. Export growth had slowed to 6.8 per cent in 2001, down from 27.8 per cent in 2000 (Reuters Asia, 2002). Following China's entry into the WTO there is likely to be more growth in foreign trade levels and freight volumes. There are estimates that by 2005, based on foreign trade of US\$ 60bn, demand for handling in the ports will reach 3bn tonnes, of which 2.2bn tonnes will go to the main ports along the coast (Cass, 2001).

The 10th five-year plan (2001-2005) of the Chinese government has been concerned with port construction and management to enhance the efficiency of ports, required to satisfy rapid economic growth and China's entry to the WTO. The plan requires new container terminals and increased capacity of existing terminals, especially the deep-water container terminals in some of the main ports in China. It also seeks to form a system of hub-and-spoke ports through developing key regional ports integrated with medium and small regional ports in a national system. Key functions of this intended system are modern information systems and ports as logistics centres (Cass, 2001).

Where does Shanghai have a Comparative Advantage over its Competitors?

The Port of Shanghai is set against a vast hinterland, containing Shanghai City, China's largest manufacturing and consuming centre, and the Yangtse River delta and corridor, the major developed economic areas in China. The port trade took a quarter of national foreign trade in 2000. Furthermore, from January to July 2001, total imports through Shanghai were up by 5.3 per cent over the same period in the previous year and total exports increased by 17.6 per cent (Shanghai Electronic Data Interchange Center, 2001).

The Port of Shanghai has been undergoing remarkable and continuous growth in container throughput in the last two decades. As illustrated by Table 11.1, the average throughput increased annually by over 25 per cent in the last decade and, if this level is maintained, Shanghai will soon be handling a quarter of all Chinese container traffic, with forecast container throughput rising to 8.5m TEU by 2005 (Cass, 2001).

What Actions can Shanghai take to Attract and Maintain Customers?

Shanghai's only unique feature is to be located in the most developed area in China, a magnet for foreign investors. This does not remove the competitive threat from other ports, and the port authority has instituted various measures, including a project in association with The World Bank Group. It is called the Shanghai Port Restructuring and Development Project and is intended to improve the productiveness of the port. This project includes:

- Formulation and implementation of an action plan for restructuring the existing port facilities on the Huangpu River to rationalise their use and move cargo operations away from the city centre, such as the project of deepening the depth of the Yangtse river, the expansion of WGQ container terminals, and the soon to come construction project of deep water container terminals at Dayangshan and Xiaoyangshan Islands.

- Provision of new and replacement cargo handling equipment for existing terminals (World Bank China Office, 2001).

Port networking with Ningbo port in the south of Shanghai and Taicang port in the North is a part of the development of the Shanghai International Shipping Centre. However, to build an international shipping centre in Shanghai, it is crucial to develop the Port of Shanghai into an important regional hub with deep-water container terminals and logistics centres providing comprehensive and sophisticated logistics services to their customers.

The Benchmarking Approach

If it is to succeed, Shanghai needs to compare itself with its more direct competitors and with leading ports of the world. Benchmarking is an effective method to draw lessons from comparison with rivals and from the experiences of leading ports such as Rotterdam and Singapore. Benchmarking, is 'the planned and structured search for industry best practices and procedures (Santhouse, 1999, p.193).

The Major Competitors of Shanghai

As stated earlier, the major competitors of Shanghai in Eastern Asia are Busan in South Korea, and certain main ports of Japan, such as Kobe, Tokyo and Yokohama. To become a transhipment hub in this region, the port authority should be aware of what competitors have done to change their status in becoming hubs.

Busan is the largest container port in South Korea and stood at third position in *Containerisation International's* league table in 2000 (Beddow, 2001) with transhipment accounting for more than 30 per cent of the total throughput of containers in early 2000 (Woodbridge, 2000a). The distinct attractions of the port are twofold. Firstly, there are deep water container terminals being constructed according to a development project. After accomplishing this project, Busan will have the capacity to accommodate 14 post-Panamax container ships simultaneously (Woodbridge, 2000a). The second is *Real Time Service*, which is a value-added service offering complete real-time access anywhere in the world, at any time, to enable customers to track and trail their shipments globally (Busan East Container Terminal, 2001)

The Japanese main ports, i.e. Tokyo, Yokohama and Kobe, are ranked within the top 30 ports in 2000. Although, the container throughput of all of these ports is less than Shanghai's in recent years, they are still fierce competitors of Shanghai. There is a successful strategy, called the core port growth plan, which could be used for reference by the Port of Shanghai. This project is to build 14-15m deep berths at 11 ports, to form the nucleus of Japan's international hub ports, which include Tokyo, Yokohama and Kobe (Takita, 1998). Each port is linked with each other and the hinterland via expressways, domestic feeders and ferryboat networks. These highly efficient distribution infrastructures not only help reduce the country's huge distribution cost, but also attract a number of shipping lines to call at these ports.

Lessons From the Successful Strategies of Rotterdam and Singapore

The locations of both ports have been fundamental to their success. Both ports qualify as leading international logistics ports, and their strategies and measures for providing logistics services are key benchmarks. As suggested by Christopher (1998), logistics and supply chain benchmarking can use the three key outcomes of success, to be 'better, faster, and cheaper', as the criteria to measure performance. MNCs manage their global supply chains by applying the basic tools of supply chain strategy, such as postponement, time compression, and flexibility and information management to reach these criteria (Schary and Skjott-Larsen 1995). A port has a part to play in the fulfilment of supply chain strategies through offering logistics resources. For example, both a distripark and an intermodal transport system help to meet the requirements of postponement, just-in-time (JIT), time compression and delivery flexibility. A teleport can contribute to supply chain information management.

Rotterdam has invested heavily in both infrastructure and superstructure. This has greatly increased the efficiency of container handling. It has created high quality distriparks where logistics service providers offer services enabling the global supply chains of MNCs to operate 'better, faster and cheaper'. Comprehensive intermodal transport networks are encouraging the establishment of door-to-door transport throughout Europe. Finally, state-of-the-art information systems transform the port into a 'smart' port, by providing various types of information including cargo information for shippers.

Similar comments can be made of Singapore. Singapore not only provides superior infrastructure and superstructure, but it also assists in managing the global supply chain for its customers. Singapore has long-established major electronic systems related to logistics and shipping. *Portnet* dates back to 1984 and has been developed over the years. It is used by shipping lines, freight forwarders, shippers and government agencies, and offers the following services: on-line booking, billing, links to *TradeNet* (see below) and government agencies, scheduling for hauliers, communications between various parties in the logistics channel including freight forwarders, hauliers, shippers and shipping lines, and cargo clearance. *TradeNet* claims to have been the first nation-wide EDI system for trade administration in the world starting in 1989. Its objective is to streamline the trading documentation process, eliminate multiple forms and, among other benefits, speed up Customs clearance by providing a link with foreign traders (Gray and Kim, 2002).

There can be little doubt that investing in the supply of logistics services at ports has supported the growth in container and cargo throughputs, and given specific ports a competitive advantage. For example, Hancock Tyre of Korea established a new European Distribution Centre of 20,000m² at Distripark Maasvlakte in the port of Rotterdam anticipating an average annual turnover of three million tyres and one million batteries through this EDC. This volume is estimated as the equivalent of an annual container throughput of 10,000 TEU (Woodbridge, 2000a).

Application of Logistics Strategies to the Port of Shanghai

The examples of Rotterdam and Singapore suggest that Shanghai should focus on the three key areas of distriparks, intermodal links and the teleport function. These are required for its stated objective of becoming a transhipment hub in its region.

Establishment of distriparks Distriparks should be within the port area or close to the port boundary, and should be connected with other modes of transport such as air, road and rail networks. An airport and seaport may be located together as with Inchon Airport in Korea, which is constructed on an island with a seaport a few miles away. For this arrangement to work effectively, both the physical and information infrastructures between seaport and airport need to be integrated. Otherwise, moving a shipment from seaport to airport over a distance of just a few kilometres can involve unloading, customs clearance, and breaking bulk at the port before it can move to the airport. Another example of close links between an airport and a seaport is the logistics centre at Schiphol Rijk in the Netherlands serving both Schiphol Airport and the port of Rotterdam (Gray and Kim, 2002). Pudong International Airport near Shanghai (one hour's drive from the city centre) has opened a new logistics centre, and has good EDI and Customs clearance systems (Export Today, 2001). A supervision centre for express parcels has also been set up at Pudong International Airport to process 7,500 parcels an hour (Xinhua News Service, 2001).

In Rotterdam and other ports the fourth generation of MIDAs (Maritime Industrial Development Areas) have attracted both heavy industry and industry based on imported goods, including high technology products which are often re-exported (Hilling and Browne, 1998). The latter development is associated with the concept of the 'free port', 'free trade zone' or 'foreign trade zone' (FTZ), which, in its most basic form, is a warehouse operating under customs bond, but may also consist of a number of factories where goods are processed and re-exported without customs duty being paid. Such zones may also undertake inventory management.

Since China has adopted reforms and open-door policies, more and more foreign corporations have been setting up business there. Consequently, the competitive environment is as intense in China as anywhere else. In fact, for many markets the competition is probably the fiercest in the world. Therefore, MNCs require a smooth, and efficient supply chain to enhance their competitive strength. To meet this requirement, setting up an integrated logistics centre has been an objective within the WGQ FTZ area close to the Shanghai Port Authority-controlled marine facilities (Fossey, 2000a). High quality logistics services may result from China's pledge to allow foreign logistics operators to operate without forming joint ventures with Chinese companies. Another example of liberalisation in the freight transport sectors is the plan to float about 35 per cent of Sinotrans to overseas investors (Hong Kong Imail, 2002).

In another case, the General Motors (GM) joint venture company in

Shanghai, Shanghai General Motors (SGM), the largest US investment project in Shanghai, has adopted just-in-time inventory management. The Ryder Logistics Company has designed a 'zero inventory' management system for SGM, building a Redistribution Centre (RDC) next to the production line to keep 288 sets of 'completely knocked-down' (CKD) kits for lowest safety inventory. Other CKDs are transported and do not occupy a large warehouse. COSCO provides door-to-door service, and is responsible for carrying CKDs from GM's Canadian distribution centre to SGM's RDC (COSCO, 2001).

This is an indication of how increasing competition between foreign and Chinese companies requires them to participate in integrated logistics management and an appropriate outsourcing system within a co-ordinated global supply chain. There can be no doubt that the first stage in setting up a world-class logistics service in the Port of Shanghai is to establish distriparks with multiple functions, close to the container terminals.

According to the requirements of the Chinese Government's programme for the Shanghai logistics industry development and the layout of the national road network, six logistics centres are to be established in Shanghai, during the period of the 10th five-year plan (2001-2005). Within these logistics centres, two logistics centres will be constructed nearby or within Shanghai Port areas. One is Waigaoqiao Logistics Centre, which includes the WGQ FTZ and the WGQ Container Terminal. Another is the Luchaogang Haigangcheng Logistics Centre, where is going to supply the logistics services for Dayangshan and Xiaoyangshan deep-water container terminals (It56, 2002).

After accession to the WTO, the procurement by MNCs in China has provided Chinese logistics service providers with more opportunities. For example, the USA based GE will increase its procurement in China to one-third of its total as a major strategy. Therefore, many cities, including Shanghai, intend to become procurement centres for MNCs. More than 200 MNCs have established their procurement divisions in Shanghai. According to a report of the Hong Kong Trade Development Council in March 2001, more than 70 per cent of overseas importers consider that Shanghai can become a competitive international procurement centre, if Shanghai is able to get co-operative relationships with MNCs directly. (Sun, 2002).

Integrated transport chain with intermodal networks Through integrated transport and an intermodal transport network, the transport chain should be as far-reaching as possible, at the same time ensuring a flexible, economical, and fast quality of service. In an effective intermodal system, ship, rail and road connections are co-ordinated at the port and inland terminals under a single door-to-door freight bill.

There are some indications that Shanghai could learn from Rotterdam in setting up intermodal networks. In the port of Rotterdam, the use of motorised and containerised barges of up to 1,000 TEUs for inland water connections could be accepted by the Chinese authorities for the Yangtse River to raise the transport capability of the river from Shanghai up to Chongqing i.e. as far as 2,400km along the river (Cargo Systems, 2000).

The port of Shanghai should concentrate on the development of intermodal rail services. In both Europe and the USA there is evidence that intermodal rail transport has enormous growth potential, both as a means of moving international maritime containers more cost-effectively and efficiently to and from the ports and in improving inter-city freight transport connections. China, with the second largest rail network in the world of more than 55,000 km of track, should develop this type of service, particularly in respect of the extensive hinterland of the Port of Shanghai (Fossey, 2000b).

Shanghai as a teleport By occupying a pivotal position in the supply chain, ports can provide substantial information on a number of types of logistics activities and resources, such as that offered by the *Real Time Service* provided by the port of Busan. To become a teleport, a port should have a Global Positioning System (GPS) network that enables customers to track and trail cargoes at all times, and a comprehensive electronic data interchange (EDI) network to improve logistics performance.

The Chinese Government is investigating the use of modern information technology to improve transport infrastructure. The MOC EDI Port Project is intended to enable key ports to conduct business using EDI with the many shippers and agencies. The project consists of the electronic linkage of 26 ocean ports and most inland ports with all the shippers using these centres, and the setting up in each of these ports of an 'EDI Centre' to which the local freight companies, agencies and shippers will be connected. These EDI Centres are also connected to each other and to government agencies such as the Customs authority. The initial phase of the project involves AMTrix-enabling for EDI (AMtrix is a messaging system for interactive EDI) at four of China's major ocean ports, Tianjin (near Beijing), Qingdao, Shanghai and Ningbo (a deep water port near

Shanghai), and COSCO, China's largest shipping line (Genex Technology, 2001).

Conclusion

This paper has attempted to analyse several important issues relating to the role played by seaports within the global supply chain, and to recommend the key strategies of logistics development for setting up logistics services in the Port of Shanghai.

The situation can be summarised as follows. Globalisation and containerisation lead to strategic alliances between global manufacturing or trading corporations and logistics service providers for global supply chain management. Shipping lines are foremost amongst the logistics service providers. At the same time, shipping lines seek economies of scale by deploying the largest possible containerships. This leads to the formation of hub-and-spoke systems within the main sea routes. Consequently, the seaports find themselves in intense competition to gain the hub position in a region. However, building a deep-water container terminal and equipping it with state-of-the-art handling facilities may not be sufficient, because ports are under increasing pressure to play a more active role in the integration of logistics, particularly from shipping lines in their role as logistics service providers.

Thus, ports are expected to be not just modal transfer points but also integrated logistics centres embedded in 'seamless' transport chains. To fulfil this role ports must develop value-added logistics activities, information systems and intermodal networks. Given these circumstances, the Port of Shanghai aims to establish an international shipping centre and become a regional hub for container shipments. Based on the example of the success of Rotterdam and Singapore, it can be concluded that there are suitable strategies that can be adopted by Shanghai. Initially, distriparks should be set up within or near container terminals and be capable of offering value-added logistics services. This should be followed by the development of an intermodal network with good connections to other modes and to the hinterland. The Port of Shanghai should keep pace with developments in EDI and e-commerce to achieve status as a world-class logistics information centre. This probably requires a specific sector of the port responsible for logistics development management. The port should not undertake such developments in isolation, but should share expertise with other ports in the Yangtse River delta, to enhance the region's overall competitive position.

References

Ashar. A. (2000) Big Can Be Beautiful, *Cargo Systems,* June, pp. 11-12.

Beddow, M. (2001) Top 30 ports, *Containerisation International,* March, p. 93.

Buck Consultants International (1997) *Europese Distributie En Aardetoevoeging Door Buitenlandse Bedrijven.* A report for Holland International Distribution Council. Nijmegen.

Busan East Container Terminal (2001) http://www.pect.co.kr.

Cao Min (2000) Consolidation and Delivery of International Container at Shanghai Port, *Containerisation,* January, pp. 23-27.

Cargo Systems (2000) China: a Cargo Systems Supplement: Bucking the Trend, November, pp. 6-9.

Carter, J. R., Pearson, J. N, and Peng, L. (1997) Logistics Barriers to International Operations: the Case of the People's Republic of China, *Journal of Business Logistics*, 18, 2, 129-145.

Cass, S. (2001) The Chinese Dragon Roars On, *Cargo Systems Supplement Top 100 Container Ports*, July, pp. 10-15.

China Business Review (2001) APEC in China: the Shanghai Model Port Project, *China Business Review*, Sept-Oct, pp. 22-26.

China Statistical Data (2002) Beijing All China Marketing Research Co. authorised by the China National Bureau of Statistics http://www.china.org.cn.

Christopher, M. (1998) *Logistics and Supply Chain Management*, Second edition, Financial Times and Pitman Publishing.

Containerisation (2002) Collection of Information, January, p.20.

COSCO (2001) http://www.cosco.com.

Deputy Director of Shanghai Informatization Office, June 6th 2000, http://unpan1.un.org/intradoc/groups/public/documents/apcity/unpan0 00292.pdf.

European Conference of Ministers of Transport (1997) *Report of the 104th Round Table on Transport Economics*, Paris, 3-4th October, 1996, ECMT, Paris.

Export Today (2001) China Outbound, *Export Today's Global Business*, 17, 1, p. 40.

Fossey, J. (2000a) Shanghai Sensation, *Containerisation International,* March, pp. 81-83.
Fossey, J. (2000b) Fast Track, *Containerisation International,* April, pp. 83-85.
Gao Huijun (2000) Prospects of China's Container Ports, *Port Economy,* First Issue, pp. 29-31.
Genex Technology (2001) Genex Technology Co., Ltd, Thailand http://www.genex.co.th.
Gray, R. and Kim, G. (2002) *Logistics and International Shipping.* Dasom Publishing, Korea.
Gu Qiangsheng, (2000) Development Research on Container Transport in Pudon, *Containerisation,* October, pp. 1-5.
Guo Xiaonan, (2000) Analysis Of Vigorous Development of Container Transport in Shanghai Port, *Containerisation,* December, pp. 17-20.
Hilling, D. and Browne, M. (1998) Ships, Ports and Bulk Freight Transport, in Hoyle, B. and Knowles, R. (eds) *Modern Transport Geography* (2nd edn) Wiley: Chichester (pp. 241-261).
Hong Kong Imail (2002) TNT Targets China in Push for Growth, *Hong Kong Imail,* 4 January 2002.
Hutchison Port Holdings (2002) www.hph.com.hk/business/ports/china/sct_fact.htm.
It56 (2002) On-line Chinese News Service http://www.it56.com.
Juhel, M. H. (1999) *The Role of Logistics in Stimulating Economic Development,* Logistics Seminar, China, Beijing, November, 28th.
Lloyd's Shipping Economist (2001) Threat of US Demand Slowdown, *Lloyd's Shipping Economist,* April, pp. 14-19.
Luo, W. (2001) *Third Party Logistics,* Shanghai Social Sciences Publishing House.
Qu Jinglinag and Han Bingquan (1999) Analysis of Growth of Container Throughput at Shanghai Container Terminal, *Containerisation,* October, pp. 14-15.
Reuters Asia (2002) http://asia.reuters.com.
Santhouse, D. (1999) Benchmarking, in Waters. D. (ed.) *Global Logistics and Distribution Planning, Strategies for Management,* Third edition, CRC Press, London, pp. 193-202.
Schary, P. B. and Skjott-Larsen, T. (1995) *Managing the Global Supply Chain,* Handelshojkolens Forlag, Copenhagen.
Shanghai Electronic Data Interchange Center (2001), http://english.21shipping.com.

Shanghai Information Office (2000) *Promoting the Application of Information Technology and Enhancing City Informatization.* Paper presented by He Shouchang.

Shanghai Port Authority (2000) *Port of Shanghai Handbook.*

Shanghai Statistics Bureau (2000) http://www.shei.gov.cn.

Shipping Gazette (2002) March 11-March 24, p.30.

Shou Jiangmin (2000) To Improve Comprehensive Throughput Capacity of Container Terminal at Shanghai Port, *Containerisation,* June, pp. 1-3.

Sun Dechi (2002) Review of China's Logistics in 2001, *Containerisation,* February, pp.1-5.

Sun Guangqi and Zhang Shiping (1999) General Review of the Chinese Shipping Policy for the Contemporary Era, *Maritime Policy and Management,* 26, 1, 93-99.

Takita, K. (1998) Ports Report: Japan Finance for Core Port Growth Plans: Hubs, *Lloyds List,* 12 June.

Transport Committee of Ningbo and Shanghai Transport University (2000), *Using the Theory of Modern Logistics to Enhance the Development of Container Transport in Ningbo,* Ningbo.

True, C. (2000) Rising in the East, *Port Development International,* September, pp.18-12.

Woodbridge, C. (2000a) Dual Hub Strategy Pays Off, *Containerisation International,* July, pp. 83-85.

World Bank (2001) *Port Reform Toolkit.* World Bank: Washington DC.

World Bank China Office (2001).
    http://www.worldbank.org.cn/English/content/shanghai-port.shtml.

World Trade Organisation (2001) http://www.wto.org.

Xinhua News Service (2001) Chinese News Agency on Web Site http://www.xinhuanet.com/english.

Zhang Yuezhong (2000) The Dragon Head, *Containerisation International,* July, pp. 75-77.

For Product Safety Concerns and Information please contact our EU representative GPSR@taylorandfrancis.com Taylor & Francis Verlag GmbH, Kaufingerstraße 24, 80331 München, Germany

Printed and bound by CPI Group (UK) Ltd, Croydon, CR0 4YY

08/05/2025

01864532-0001